GOOD ENOUGH

A Career Woman's Guide to Confidence,
Courage and Credibility

Jo Painter

CRANTHORPE
MILLNER

A CIP catalogue record for this title is available from the British Library.

ISBN 978-1-912964-16-1 (Paperback)

www.cranthorpemillner.com

First Published (2020)

Cranthorpe Millner Publishers

To all the amazing women who allowed me the privilege of hearing their stories and supporting them on their journey to change. To my wonderful family, Mike, Holly and Jake, who no longer have to hear me say, "Sorry I can't, I'm just writing my book!"

About the Author

Jo Painter is a leading international career, leadership and confidence coach. She originally qualified as a pharmacist and her career began in a FTSE 100 company where for 17 years she had a very successful corporate career.

Jo soon made the decision to combine her qualifications in and love of coaching with her corporate experiences to support other women and help them achieve their career dreams.

She has researched, studied and worked with thousands of career women over the last twelve years. As an expert in the field of women's career success she has appeared on Sky News, worked with PR agencies, appears regularly in the media and is a sought-after keynote speaker with companies such as Amazon, Ford and Lloyds Bank.

She lives in Bishop's Stortford with her husband, children and dog.

Introduction

Chapter 1

Why Don't I Feel Good Enough? 10

Chapter 2

'Nice Girl' Conditioning 21

Chapter 3

The Inner Critical Parrot 30

Chapter 8

Chapter 9

Chapter 10

Chapter 11

I'm Okay, You're Okay: How to be Assertive..... 151

Chapter 12

Having That Difficult Conversation and Dealing with Conflict 169

Chapter 15

Chapter 16

Introduction

"I'm worried I'm not Good Enough."
"What if they don't think I'm Good Enough?"
"They're going to find out I'm not Good Enough."

These statements and questions regularly come up in discussions with my clients. Why is it that so many women like us feel that we aren't Good Enough at work?

As women, we have all the capabilities and attributes needed for leadership and senior management. We possess powerful problem-solving abilities, empathy, ethics, and tend to be great team-players, motivators and role models.

But, for many, our level of self-belief and our courage to take risks doesn't reflect these valuable skills.

In my role as a Career, Leadership and Confidence Coach, I see many immensely talented and incredibly accomplished women who won't stop doubting themselves.

Perhaps you're one of them?

Do you feel under pressure to prove yourself? Have you fallen into habitual behaviours that keep you stuck? Does it feel like a battle with your inner critic to keep delivering your unrealistic standards?

Well, the good news is change is absolutely possible.

I'd love to be able to hand you a magic wand which with one flick would ensure you always felt genuinely Good Enough.

I'm afraid though that like most things worth having it takes commitment, intention and practice. If you can provide those, then this book will give you the rest.

In the 12 years I've spent researching successful women and working with hundreds of amazing clients, I've discovered the typical biases and challenges that women face at work. These can be cultural, like an unconscious bias towards men or when a woman who is very self-confident gets a backlash for being thought of as aggressive or bossy.

Then there are the individual challenges such as the Imposter Syndrome – worrying you're not Good Enough for the job and you'll be found out, or the fear of being judged negatively by others which makes you think you need to deliver at a perfect level all the time.

As you explore this book, you'll read about these challenges, but the focus will be on the proven strategies my clients have used to overcome them. You will also find inspiring real-life stories from the awesome women I have worked with.

What is the Confidence Gap?

The idea of 'The Confidence Gap' between men and women at work became universally accepted around 2013/2014. It was around this time that books such as Sheryl Sandberg's *Lean In* [i]and *The Confidence Code* by Katty Kay and Claire Shipman[ii] were popular.

The low number of women in senior leadership positions was thought to be a result of this confidence gap.

Both books provided research and studies to support this theory. One of the most well-known studies in *The Confidence Code* took place with Hewlett Packard employees. They analysed internal data relating to when candidates felt confident enough to apply for promotions.

Women working at Hewlett Packard, the study discovered, applied for a promotion only when they believed they met almost 100 per cent of the qualifications listed for the job. Men were happy to put themselves forward when they thought they could achieve 60 per cent of the job requirements.

From this, it was surmised that women hold themselves back from applying as they lack confidence in their abilities and fear the outcome if they fail.

There have been many other studies backing this assumption. In 2014 an American consulting company published a report called *Everyday Moments of Truth: Frontline Managers Are Key to Women's Career Aspirations*[iii]. It found that 43% of women aspire to senior management when they start working for a company but only 27% have the confidence to actually do so. After two years of employment, this confidence figure drops to a low 13%.

Whereas, 28% of men start out being confident they can reach senior management, and after two years of experience, 55% of them believe they can achieve that top role.

The suggestions that came out of the report were about line managers recognising a balance of skills in an individual rather than just the existing leadership competences, and the importance of balanced recruitment processes and support from the boardroom.

The confidence gap has been the subject of an overwhelming number of articles. The majority of them conclude that women have less self-belief and are more risk averse than men.

Before I go further, I would like to point out that despite everything I've said so far, this book is not about telling women to pull themselves together and behave 'like a man'. There are many interwoven issues involved in finding a solution to the lack of top-level women, but blaming women or men is certainly not the answer.

In the years following the release of the highly successful books above, many researchers have challenged the belief that women lack confidence compared to men at work.

Defining what confidence is and how it can be measured is the first problem. A study by Simmons University, *Women and Confidence: An Alternative Understanding of the 'Confidence Gap'* [iv]asks how we can know what confidence looks like. In particular, how can you see the distinction between high and low confidence when individuals demonstrate it in different ways.

The study above also says that women shouldn't be encouraged to emulate the behaviours of men. This is because firstly, not all men think and behave the same way, and secondly, women need to be authentically confident and not feel they should copy the style of others. Somehow we have given women the idea that their confidence is broken and needs to be fixed. This is not only wrong but unhelpful and can further knock women's self-belief.

In 2018, Laura Guillen, Assistant Professor of Organisational Behaviour at The European School of Management and Technology, researched the subject of self-confidence appearance along with colleagues Margarita Mayo of IE business school and Natalia Karelaia of INSEAD. They didn't focus on how confident women feel, instead, the focus was on how confident men and women *appear*.

They published the research paper, *Appearing self-confident and getting credit for it: Why it may be easier for men than women to gain influence at work* [v]

Its findings were that the consequences of appearing self-confident were not the same for women as for men. They suggested that confident men become liked and successful, whereas women who demonstrate confidence, also need to show warmth and caring if they are to be successful and fit in.

Changing this double standard can only be achieved through organisational and cultural reforms around recruitment, career progression and role models. To do this, we need more women at the boardroom table.

With the recent evolution of the #MeToo phenomenon, there is even more focus on the behaviours of men and women in the workplace. It brings a fantastic opportunity to increase the speed of change in workplace gender equality.

Whether the lack of women in senior roles is a result of low self-belief or a cultural double standard, on an individual basis, we can all agree that building your confidence will have a positive impact on your career progression.

Who Am I?

My career journey started when I qualified as a Pharmacist. I quickly realised I didn't find the profession fulfilling and instead chose the management career pathway in a FTSE 100 company.

I had a very successful 17-year corporate career, and as part of it, I got to coach the senior leaders in the business. I have always had a love of learning, and developing my coaching skills opened up a fabulous new arena for me to continually learn while supporting others to grow.

Seeing colleagues having '*Ahah!*' moments or insights into other perspectives, gave me real pleasure and a sense of achievement. I recognised that for me, coaching was fulfilling and it gave me a sense of purpose.

The role required me to stay away from home, and as I'd had my daughter, I took the option of voluntary redundancy. I used the opportunity to gain further qualifications in coaching and set up my coaching business.

I then had one of the toughest times in my life. I was diagnosed with a rare form of cancer in the placenta of my third pregnancy.

The cancer wasn't initially diagnosed, and as I was bleeding heavily, I thought I'd miscarried. The tumour was deceiving me though. The placenta produces HCG (Human Chorionic Gonadotropin), which is the hormone detected in pregnancy tests. As my tumour had taken over the placenta, this hormone was produced at extremely high levels. That meant I had all the pregnancy symptoms but multiplied.

A couple of weeks later I had a life-threatening bleed and was hospitalised. I was rushed to a specialist hospital in London as the HCG levels had rung alarm bells and the next morning I was started on chemotherapy.

The treatment led to eighteen months in a cancer bubble, where the outside world didn't seem to exist. After a horrendous time spent having chemotherapy every week for six months, regularly going neutropenic (no white blood cells for immunity) and missing out on time with my one and three-year-old, I was lucky enough to go into remission and have been clear ever since.

Coming out of this period I knew I should be happy and look forward to a new future. However, I found my confidence had crumbled, and I questioned my future purpose.

I returned to my love of coaching and began to use my coaching skills a small step at a time. While I rebuilt both my physical strength and my confidence, I also started the journey to find my new career.

It was then I had my 'light bulb' moment and realised that I wanted to help other women build their confidence and reach their potential. I decided to combine my corporate experience and the research I'd done into successful women to focus on confidence in career women and my business took off.

After 12 years of studying and working with thousands of women, I have a proven system to support women to achieve confidence, courage and credibility in their career. I'm so excited to be sharing it with you in this book.

I'm passionate about supporting wonderful women like you to achieve individual career success, as well as becoming role models for my daughter and for all the girls to come.

How to Use This Book

The purpose of this book is to raise your awareness of the challenges and opportunities that career women face, to give you an understanding of the mindset behind your behaviours and to share proven tools and strategies to help you feel confident, courageous and credible in the workplace.

Some or all of the topics in the book may apply to you. You can choose to work your way through the chapters in order, or dip in and out of the challenges that resonate with you.

I have written the book so that the first six chapters focus on the mindsets that tend to hold women back in their careers and how to overcome them. The second part of the book then builds on practical strategies to accelerate your career progression and fulfilment.

In each chapter, you'll find a 'Self-Coaching Activity', a 'Client Story' and an 'In A Nutshell' summary. I suggest at the end of each chapter that you take the time to complete the activity, and to reflect on how to put the ideas into action in your career before moving onto the next subject.

Read on, learn lots and enjoy.

Chapter 1

Why Don't I Feel Good Enough?

"When you know you're ENOUGH!
When you stop focusing on all things that you're not.
When you stop fussing over perceived flaws.
When you remove all imposed and unbelievable
expectations on yourself.
When you start celebrating yourself more.
When you focus on all that you are.
When you start believing that your perceived flaws are
just that - perception..."
Malebo Sephodi

In the introduction, I talked about confidence levels and the confidence gap between men and women. When it comes to feeling Good Enough though, there is another element, as important as your confidence.

That is your self-worth, which is a measure of how you feel about yourself and your value in the world.

If you struggle with believing you are worthy, then you may feel confident in your abilities to do your job, but still think that you are not Good Enough to be doing it.

Self-worth is something we are all born with. From our beginning, there are no feelings of inadequacy, no worrying about being judged or being compared negatively to others.

Have you ever known a baby to need counselling?

It's only over time that our thinking about the experiences we encounter changes this.

The Golden Nugget

Imagine your self-worth as a golden nugget (bear with me on this metaphor). As you experience life and have anxious thoughts about those experiences, you start to bury the nugget under a layer of soil.

The more self-doubting thoughts you have, the more layers of soil you put over your golden nugget, until you don't even remember it was a golden nugget!

When your golden nugget of self-worth gets hidden under these layers of mud and soil (our thoughts and beliefs), you lose touch with it. Then instead of knowing that you are worthy and of value, you begin to question yourself. You believe the thoughts that tell you that you're not Good Enough or as important as others.

As individuals, we don't want people to see this side of ourselves – the vulnerable, not Good Enough parts we all think we have. Which means we instead choose to wrap that mud-covered golden nugget, in a thin layer of gold paper.

That layer is your outer persona, the mask you put on to look like a real golden nugget and show others how happy and sorted you are, but it is only paper thin.

Now you are even further from your golden nugget, and it's even more difficult to touch that innate feeling of wellbeing, wisdom or gut intuition.

> *All the time, your feeling of self-worth, well-being or value is right there within you, if only you could get through the paper and mud layers.*

There are a lot of small and insignificant experiences in life that distance us from our self-worth.

For example; a simple "and what do you do?" can make us question our value and believe we only matter if we pass certain conditions. As Stanford psychologist Meag-gan O'Reilly says in her TEDx talk[vi], we then think our sense of worth depends on something outside of us.

> *What if your intrinsic value came from you just existing, rather than what you contributed or achieved?*

I remember when I first started my corporate career, it was my pre-registration year. That's a year of practical training following your degree before you can register to practise as a pharmacist.

There was another pre-registration student employed in the same area as me. He was an extrovert, charismatic and, to use an old-fashioned phrase, 'full of himself'. I've never been described as shy or an introvert, but it was my first proper job, and I had to prove myself to pass the qualification. Unsurprisingly, I was nervous and keen to make a good impression.

Instead of blossoming and thriving in the learning environment, I started to compare myself to my fellow student. While I felt I was equally, if not more, competent than him, I noticed that he was able to talk confidently about himself and focused more on building relationships within the company than on getting his qualification.

The more his profile rose, the more I doubted myself and my feelings of inadequacy grew. I became resentful that he was doing so well and I withdrew from a lot of the banter at work, becoming a quieter version of myself. I piled buckets of soil on my golden nugget of self-worth and lost sight of it.

With hindsight, this self-sabotaging behaviour came from a need to feel I fitted in and to feel Good Enough. The reality was that it left me with the feeling that I wasn't as valuable or worthy as others, and that led to self-destructive behaviours which I took a long time to overcome.

The sad thing is if I'd recognised my value and worth, I would have realised they were not based on how anyone else behaved or anything outside of me. Then I would have been able to focus on being the best version of me that I could be.

How do you recognise your self-worth?

When you lose touch with your self-worth, it feels uncomfortable, and you might start to look for things outside of you to change that feeling.

In terms of your career, that might be approval from others, climbing the career ladder or outperforming colleagues. In life you might use alcohol, food, relationships or exercise to feel better emotionally.

All of these things will give you a short-term buzz. In the longer term, to feel better in your career, you will need to keep on succeeding, and that can lead to perfectionism, Imposter Syndrome and a poor work/life balance.

If you knew your self-worth was always there, then it wouldn't matter if you got that promotion, if you have the highest sales or reach the top score on your performance review. Your inherent value would be just the same.

To understand what it feels like to be connected to that feeling of self-worth, think about a time when you were so absorbed in an activity or in the present moment that you didn't notice time passing. It could be that you were researching a new project, debating an issue you were interested in or leading a team meeting. That feeling of everything being okay and sense of achievement is what I call being '*in flow*'. Try to capture the feeling and you will be able to recognise when you're feeling Good Enough.

Imagine what would happen if you believed you were as worthy and of as much value as anyone else.

Try this simple exercise – called the 'second half of the sentence'.

Say to yourself:

"If I believed I was Good Enough I would…"

How would you finish that sentence? For example: "If I believed I was Good Enough I would apply for that promotion." Or, "If I believed I was Good Enough I wouldn't worry what other people thought about me."

Write down your first answer then ask yourself the same question repeatedly. Write down each new answer. At some point, you will find a solution that resonates with you (it can take 30 to 40 answers before you get there!).

This answer could be the message that will motivate you to accept that you are genuinely okay at any moment. Or it could be the real fear you have that stops you feeling valuable and of worth.

Am I making the right decisions?

It can feel more comfortable to let others take responsibility for decisions, especially the hard ones. When you make decisions for yourself though, you grow your self-worth and connect to that feeling of what is right for you.

> *In my experience, if a decision comes with an uncomfortable feeling, an urgency or anxiety, then your mind isn't in the best place to be making that decision.*

Your gut feeling usually comes when your mind is calm, and it arrives with a sense of, "Of course, that's what I need to do". You've probably heard of people having big ideas in the shower or bath or when walking the dog. That's because the mind is quiet enough for you to listen to your intuition or creativity.

Client Story: Sarah

I first met Sarah at one of my talks in London. I'd been presenting on the subject of self-promotion and how important it is to be visible in your career.

Sarah asked me about strategies for speaking up to her seniors when she felt intimidated by them. We had a brief chat and arranged a call to explore the subject more.

Sarah was an accountant in financial services and had been told she's very competent but needs to have more confidence and impact. During our chat, I could immediately tell that her issue was less about self-confidence in her abilities and more about believing she was worth listening to and had something of value to say.

As I've explained, not seeing your intrinsic value will affect all areas of your life and for Sarah, it was most apparent in her career, but it also affected her social life.

She told me how it was stopping her from interacting with valuable clients and senior managers. She would avoid phone calls and do as much of her interactions as possible by email.

Speaking up on conference calls with clients or internally was almost impossible for Sarah, unless she felt the client was of a similar level to her or it involved her internal colleagues.

She knew she had the knowledge to join or lead the conversations, but her lack of belief in her value and the constant thought, "Why would anyone want to listen to me?" held her back. She was using her manager or a more experienced colleague to shield her from having to put herself forward. She'd ensure they led the calls and handled the questions.

Not only did her line manager point this out as a development issue, but Sarah was extremely frustrated with herself about it. By this point it had built into a habit she was unable to change.

As a coach, I could have helped Sarah set realistic goals and challenged her to speak up on every call. I realised though that there was a deeper issue involved and we agreed to start building her self-worth before she tried to conquer her fears about speaking up.

Sarah had an older sister who was an extrovert and extremely gregarious. Sarah however was more of an introvert, preferring one to one situations, and was uncomfortable if the focus was on her.

While she loved her sister and her outgoing behaviour, it had meant that as a child she was dominated by her and often pushed by adults to be more like her, which resulted in her withdrawing and feeling not Good Enough.

We began Sarah's coaching by focusing on changing her mindset around how she thinks of herself. Raising her awareness of her positives, her contribution to work and life, her values and the power she has just from existing.

I asked Sarah to focus on listening to herself – her wants and needs and opinions. To start making decisions for herself rather than following what others want or decide.

Building self-worth is a journey, not a quick flick of a switch, and so it was an ongoing focus throughout Sarah's programme. As she started to change her perception of herself, we looked at practical strategies to help her feel and demonstrate confidence. You'll find some of these strategies in the following chapters.

Sarah has since moved job – something she'd never have considered before our coaching. She has more responsibility and has crushed those 'speaking up gremlins'.

Self-Coaching Activity

If you believe self-worth is something you'd like to build, then start by focusing on changing your perception of yourself. As busy women, we rarely spend time thinking about our positives and our value.

Here are a few exercises to help alter your perspective. They may seem simple but can be harder than you expect. Put aside your modesty and dig deep.

1. **List 10 things you like about yourself.** They can be physical attributes, behaviours, qualities, talents, small or big.

2. **List 10 things you have achieved in the last ten years**. They can be small or big; they can be around your career, education, social life, hobbies or family. Remember an achievement doesn't mean you have to have had a real struggle to get there.

3. **Ask three work colleagues and three personal contacts to name your strengths**. What others think are our positives can be surprising. Ask each person to name three words that describe your strengths. Try to ask people who aren't as easy to approach, such as people you don't know well or you feel intimidated by, rather than your close friends and family. You're more likely to get useful and unexpected feedback from them.

4. **When do you feel in flow?** Earlier in the chapter I mentioned that when we feel 'in flow' we are connected with our self-worth and time flies by. We are also usually doing something we enjoy and are good at. When do you get this experience at work? Try to imagine the feeling now and become aware of what you are doing when a sense of fulfilment appears again.

5. **Do you treat yourself with the same care, tolerance and compassion that you would to a close friend?** If not then be aware of the way you talk to yourself, in your mind or to others. Try to avoid negative self-talk even if it's as a joke as those words will reinforce your low self-worth and confidence.

In A Nutshell

- Self-worth is a measure of how you feel about yourself and your place in the world.
- We're all born with the same self-worth, and it's our thoughts about our experiences in life that distance us from the golden nugget of self-worth.
- Our feeling of value comes from inside us and not from a promotion, a bigger pay packet or someone else's validation.
- Once you accept and believe you are Good Enough, you are free to become the best version of yourself.
- Focus on your positives, strengths, and talents. What is important to you and what fulfils you?

Chapter 2

'Nice Girl' Conditioning

"To be nobody-but-yourself — in a world which is doing its best, night and day, to make you everybody else — means to fight the hardest battle which any human being can fight."
E. E. Cummings

What do I mean by 'nice girl' conditioning?

'Nice Girl' conditioning results from the messages we pick up as a child from parents, schools and society about how you 'should' behave.

These ideas that we absorb with a child's mind may not have been intended to give that message. If we internalise them as rules we must follow in life, despite being illogical to an adult's mind, they can hold us back.

For example, were you told as a child to:

- Be a good girl

- Be polite

- Put others first

- Be humble

21

- Never 'blow your own trumpet'

- Never disagree or upset people

- Respect your elders and betters

While good manners are important and understandably something to teach your children, living your life by someone else's standards or by what you perceived to be their expectation as a child only stops you from being authentic and doing what's right for you. It also knocks your self-worth.

Girls, and sometimes boys, are given the message in school to be good, work hard and fit in. Get high exam results and good reports, because then you will receive praise, validation and gold stars. In contrast, boys tend to be encouraged to challenge rules and be adventurous. Although this isn't true of everyone, it's certainly a pattern I see in my clients.

The type of 'nice girl' messages my clients have told me about include:

"You have to succeed to get love and security."

"It's not nice to talk yourself up; you'll sound like a bragger."

"I need to listen and agree with people who have more seniority, knowledge or experience."

"Always help others and never say No."

"It's selfish to put your needs before someone else."

These types of messages put layers of soil over your golden nugget of self-worth and as we go through life, we look for evidence to back up these rules or messages we have picked up.

You have probably experienced a situation where you've looked for evidence of something being real, and so you can't help but find it.

For example, if you think your boss is disappointed in you, you'll spend the day observing them until you see them engrossed in a chat with a colleague or not looking your way. Then you take this as evidence of their annoyance rather than normal behaviour.

When you find this evidence, it will reinforce the rules you picked up as a child. That leads you subconsciously to turn your self-imposed regulations into beliefs that limit how you behave and what you can achieve.

Am I Good Enough as a leader?

If you put others first, worry about upsetting people and don't see your value in the workplace, you are more likely to be seen as a safe pair of hands in your current role rather than having the potential and visibility to progress as a leader.

Society's view of what a leader looks like has made some steps forward in the last decade. However, in many companies and industries, it is still seen as a middle-aged white male, who is decisive, extroverted and bold.

Changing this stereotype requires a huge change in a multitude of other issues, such as unconscious bias towards males and against women, the gender pay gap, recruitment processes, promotion requirements and women feeling Good Enough.

In this book, I've kept the focus on women valuing themselves and their abilities, while still highlighting the other challenges.

At the beginning of the book, I mentioned the particular strengths of women: empathy, problem-solving, collaboration and relationship building. If we compare these with the characteristics of the stereotypical leader, it's clear that women will be handicapped by not valuing their additional strengths.

I'm sure you can see the contrast between that stereotypical picture of a leader with the 'nice girl' I've described. As a result, the likelihood of getting noticed for your potential and achieving career progression drops further.

Have you taken on board this type of conditioning?

If you have then you will probably find it uncomfortable to deal with confrontation or challenge seniors. Other challenges you may have are speaking up if you are not 100% sure you are right and sharing your career successes.

I grew up in a mainly traditional family environment. My dad worked fixed hours and came home at the same time every night to the tea my mum had prepared. She was a homemaker and never worked again after having my twin older brothers.

When my dad wasn't working, he was doing DIY around the house and Mum would be busy sewing clothes, baking or working for the Samaritans.

I look back and feel great warmth for having had a happy and secure middle-class childhood. I do think, however, that the different expectations of men and women definitely shaped the paths that my brothers and I followed.

The messages I got subconsciously from my family were that the big decisions, the purse strings and the person to be respected were the males. As a female, we should be the one to smooth things over, to put others first and to compromise on our wants and needs.

I have a very clear memory of one of many occasions when my dad shouted at one of my brothers for bad behaviour. We were eating a family meal, and my brother stole potatoes off my plate and managed to drop them on the floor.

My dad angrily blew up and told my brother to get outside, which he refused to do. As a parent, I can resonate with the frustration my dad must have felt. It drove him to eventually drag my brother away from the table.

The reason I mention this story is because of the reaction I had to the situation. I was upset at my dad's behaviour, but the strongest emotion I had was of feeling hurt and scared for my brother. That gave me the physical feeling of extreme nausea and churning in my stomach.

From then on if I was ever told off (and my dad only needed to look at me sternly), the same feeling came back. I had internalised a fear of being told off, and to avoid it I developed some 'nice girl' behaviours.

Looking back on my career I can see in the early years I was a people pleaser and overly respectful towards anyone in seniority. I was lucky enough to have this pointed out to me by a very supportive manager and was able to build my confidence, but it took me years of hard work to get there.

Although family life today is far less conventional, those unconscious biases in how we raise children are still around.

I find myself reacting to some of my son's behaviours towards his friends as, 'he's just being a teenage boy'. Whereas, if my daughter did something similar, I would be shocked that she wasn't being 'nice' to her friends.

This imbalance in our expectations of boys and girls does affect how comfortable they are with certain behaviours later in life. It was undoubtedly an issue for my client Helen.

Client Story: Helen

Helen is a partner in a London law firm. She's had a successful career so far and is looking to progress to senior partner. She has a young family and together with her husband balances her career and home life.

Helen contacted me as she knew that her success so far had been down to hard work and excellent results. To get to the next level, she now needed to demonstrate real confidence, get her voice heard and influence her seniors.

She'd had feedback that she was too 'nice' and needed to 'sharpen her shoulders'. Not the most helpful of advice, but the underlying message was that she needed to have more impact.

In particular, Helen tended to allow a senior partner in her area to speak for her in internal meetings and with valuable clients. Her behaviour came from the belief that she must respect her 'elders and betters', something that was ingrained in her subconscious, along with her fear of saying something stupid or having her opinion judged negatively. This had led to Helen covering her golden nugget of self-worth with layers of doubt.

For Helen to make a change, it meant challenging her fear of upsetting others and her firm belief that people with greater seniority or experience were better than her.

Through our coaching, Helen realised that a lot of her beliefs about herself and the world had come from her mum. Her mother was a loving and dominant figure in her life and had always been concerned about what other people thought of their family.

This belief had led her to instil in her children a need to please others and not share your real thoughts, wants and needs.

To challenge and change these beliefs, Helen needed to step out of the role of 'nice' child and into a competent adult role.

We went over the evidence that backed up her belief that she was not equal to her 'elders and betters', that if she said the wrong thing, she would look stupid or be rejected.

Was there any evidence that this has ever happened?

If so, what was the result, and was it as bad as she thought?

From there Helen developed a new belief to replace the old one. A belief that she found kind and realistic. For her this was:

"I'm in the meeting or the conversation because they want to hear my opinion."

And:

"If people don't agree with what I share, nothing awful will happen, and I will have valued myself by voicing my opinion."

I'd love to say this changed Helen's self-belief overnight, but of course it's something that takes time. What it did do was create a shift in her perception of her value.

I encouraged her to get her voice heard in difficult situations, taking it a small step at a time. We identified the conditions she felt uncomfortable in and focused on a specific intention for that circumstance. Such as asking a question, adding her opinion on a particular discussion and gradually building her confidence up, so that today she can speak up without thinking about it.

Self-Coaching Activity

Being aware of the limiting beliefs or rules like 'nice girl' conditioning that you have is the first step to diluting their power.

1. What messages did you pick up through your childhood that may be limiting you to just being a 'nice girl'?
2. Think about where you picked them up – was that the message your parents, teacher etc. meant?
3. What would be a logical, kind and realistic message to replace it?
4. In what situations at work does this 'nice girl' limitation hold you back?
5. If you permitted yourself to take a step away from all the rules a 'nice girl' would follow, what is the first thing you'd do?

In A Nutshell

- Conditioning from childhood and society can result in you believing you must stick to a specific set of rules or behaviours and be a 'nice girl'.
- Expectations of boys and girls can affect self-belief and make it uncomfortable for you to speak up or deal with stressful situations.
- Internalising these beliefs can hold you back in your career.
- By being aware of and challenging these beliefs, you can change your mindset and have 'permission' to change your behaviour.

When you're ready, move onto the next chapter.

Chapter 3

The Inner Critical Parrot

"Even our worst enemies don't talk about us the way we speak to ourselves. I call this voice the obnoxious roommate living in our head. It feeds on putting us down and strengthening our insecurities and doubts."
Arianna Huffington

The Inner Critic is that voice that we all have in our heads telling us we are not Good Enough, we are not capable of our goals or we will mess up. It is a self-destructive voice whose dialogue is behind a lot of our self-sabotaging behaviour.

According to psychologist Rick Hanson, author of 'How to Stand Up To Your Inner Critic',[vii] we all have two different voices inside us: one that is nurturing and one that is critical; one that lifts, and one that weighs us down. Both of these voices have a role to play. Our inner nurturer brings self-compassion and encouragement and comes from that core of self-worth that we all have, while the inner critic helps you recognise where you've gone wrong and what you need to do to put things right.

The problem is that the inner critic seems to shout a lot louder than the nurturer and doesn't stick to only talking about things that have gone wrong. Your inner critic is also an expert at judging, criticising and demeaning you, whether what it says is true or not.

This constant negative dialogue can chip away at your self-worth and resilience and can cause you to play small. If your inner critic is highly active, then its effects can be debilitating on your confidence and career progression.

In the next few chapters, I will be covering the perfectionist mindset, imposter syndrome and the tendency to compare yourself to others. All of these are driven by that inner critical voice speaking up and reminding you that you are not Good Enough.

The good news is that you can either turn down the volume on your critic or use it as a motivational tool.

What does your inner critic say?

In my years of working with clients to build their confidence and self-worth, I have witnessed a massive number of inner critical statements, and these are a few of the popular ones:

"You're not Good Enough."

"If you speak up they will think you're stupid."

"People like you aren't successful."

"Who do you think you are to do that?"

"You'll just mess up again."

"Why would anyone want to speak to you?"

Don't they all sound horrible? Can you believe this is what we are saying to ourselves?

The inner critic can also be cleverly comforting and manipulative too:

"You're fine in your job, don't go pushing yourself for promotion, it's too stressful."

"You deserve a glass of wine; you have worked really hard."

"Your boss will never give you a pay rise, so there is no point in asking."

Other people hear a critical voice that makes them feel like a victim:

"It's not fair; none of them works as hard as me."

"You are under too much pressure, why don't they give you more support?"

"I deserved that promotion; it was a fix from the start."

Do any of these sound like your inner critic?

My inner critic particularly likes the, "Why would anyone want to speak to you?" and, "You deserve a glass of wine" quotes. I know they are just thoughts, but I can still get caught up in believing them.

> **This concept of an inner critical voice has developed as part of modern psychology. The voice is only a thought, not an inner guru or moral code that you must listen to.**

As you will hear me say throughout this book, you don't need to be scared of a thought. It has no power over you, is probably not true and you don't need to engage with it.

I appreciate that the thoughts are loud, distracting and feel real, but they have no control over you unless you choose to believe and act on them. We all have free will to make that choice.

The 7 Types of Inner Critic

Psychologists <u>Jay Earley, Ph.D., and Bonnie Weiss, LCSW,</u>[viii] have described the seven types of Inner Critic in their book, *The 7 Types of Inner Critic*. Do you recognise yourself in any of them?

Type 1: The Perfectionist

This type of inner critic will always set incredibly high (often impossible) standards for you to reach. The theme for this inner critic is always around perfection. For example, the focus on perfection could be around your work, your appearance or your relationships. According to this inner critic, if you are not doing things perfectly, then you are at risk of not fitting in, which is a fearful place to be, because that may mean you could be judged or rejected.

Tip – having realistic expectations, rather than setting yourself up to fail, is the best antidote to this inner critic.

Type 2: The Inner Controller

An inner controller is a hard and shaming voice focused on controlling your impulses. Your impulses can range from anything to do with your eating or drinking or your working hours. The fear for this inner critic is that you could lose control at any moment, so it shames you into controlling your behaviour so that you can come across as a 'good' person.

Tip – what would happen if you did let go? Is the fear that you would really become an alcoholic or work so little that you would get fired really a legitimate one?

Type 3: The Taskmaster

As you might expect, the Taskmaster is determined to make you work as hard as possible. Success at all costs is the goal. This inner critical voice will become very outspoken if you slow down or take a break. Laziness is out of the question. According to this inner critic, if you aren't pushing yourself and striving for more, you are failing.

Tip – put boundaries in place for your working hours and try taking an hour out of your time outside work to do nothing, relax, listen to music or read.

Type 4: The Underminer

This inner critic will do anything to undermine your self-confidence in an effort to stop you from taking any risks. The Underminer believes that playing it small is the safest place to be. Any attempt to rise, be visible, or simply be big, is seen as a threat, and it will do anything to prevent that from happening.

Tip – challenge yourself to take a small step outside your comfort zone at work. Volunteer for a small extra responsibility or talk about a success you and your team had.

Type 5: The Destroyer

This dangerous inner critic aims to make you believe you are never Good Enough. No matter what you do, you are intrinsically flawed. It will consistently attack your level of self-worth and stop you from accepting that you're okay as you are. That leads to continually seeking ways to 'fix' or improve yourself.

Tip – try to accept that we are all okay as we are. If you want to develop further yourself, that is great, but you don't need *fixing*. Remember your golden nugget of self-worth is always there for you to connect with.

Type 6: The Guilt-Tripper

The Guilt-Tripper brings up the past at any opportunity that it can. It will harbour resentments and is unable to forgive you or others for any problematic experiences that may have led to pain. It believes that to stop the past from repeating itself, it must remind you of it at all times.

Tip – choose to distract yourself from painful memories from the past. They have no benefit to you and are often exaggerated by your imagination. By letting go of mistakes others have made, you stop being the only person hurt.

Type 7: The Conformist

This type of inner critic will try to get you to conform to your family or to society's standards so that you will be admired and loved. If you step slightly out of line, it will speak up so that you don't 'rock the boat'. If you're not conforming, it thinks you're at risk of being rejected.

Tip – question the 'rules' to which you stick. Where did they come from, and do you still want to adhere to them?

All of these internal voices sound brutally harsh, but the intention of the inner critic is actually to try and protect you from a perceived emotional threat.

How do I quieten down the sound of my inner critic?

It is possible to turn down the volume on your inner critic and alter the imbalance between your inner critic and inner nurturer. Here are some steps to get you started:

1. **Become aware of the situations where your inner critical voice speaks up**.

Is it when you feel unsure of your abilities, when the focus turns to you or perhaps when you try something new? Pay attention to where it happens and notice if there are any themes that connect the situations. Do this with curiosity rather than looking for a way to be self-critical.

2. Listen to the words your inner critic says and what it wants you to do

The exact words you hear can give you a clue to the source of your critical voice. Make a note of the different statements you hear. Is it a similar phrase that you hear repeatedly, or does the criticism vary? Again listen from a place of curiosity and interest, not judgement.

Try these examples to help you get tuned in.

a. *Imagine that you're in a meeting with people you don't know well, including some very senior leaders. You disagree with the idea being discussed and have a different suggestion you'd like to explore, but your inner critic is holding you back.*

   What is the inner critic in your head saying?

b. *Imagine you're about to start working with colleagues on a project. They have specific expertise in areas you don't know much about, and you're worried about the value you can add.*

   What does your inner critic say?

Now you know what your inner critical voice is saying, can you work out what it wants you to do or to avoid doing?

Is it trying to keep you small and not take a risk? Could it be trying to keep you exactly where you are in your job or life? Or is it looking to get rid of the bad feelings that are making you uncomfortable?

3. Who or what does your inner critic sound like?

Clients will often tell me that their inner critical voice sounds like their parents, a teacher or an old boss. The benefit of attaching a person or character to the voice is that it detaches the critical words from you.

You may have wondered why I called this chapter, 'The Inner Critical Parrot'. That is because I think of my inner critical voice as a parrot squawking away on my shoulder. When I talk about this in my presentations and workshops, I have a large, colourful parrot that actually does squawk. My clients have characterised their inner critics as all sorts of things, including cartoon villains, Gollum from Lord of The Rings or Cruella De Vil.

Choosing a funny character works for me, as I can then observe its harshness and illogical attitude from a distance. As the character is outside of me, and I am not personally identifying with it, I no longer reinforce it's words. Stripping away the power from my negative voice means I can hear it, but not be it.

4. Turn to your Inner Nurturer

The inner nurturer is the compassionate and supportive internal voice that comes from your golden nugget of self-worth and is developed from the loving behaviours of your parents and other primary carers. Thinking of yourself as a child or someone needing protection and encouragement can override your inner critic and build confidence and resilience.

Use your inner nurturer to challenge what your critic has said. You have already identified the words it uses, now think of one or two examples that contradict that opinion.

With my example, "Why would anyone want to speak to you?" I can argue that I am regularly asked to speak to organisations and most will invite me back. I have a high percentage of clients that return to me for second programmes on new issues.

If your inner critic says, "You are going to mess up again" you can challenge it with examples of when you haven't messed up or ask yourself - where did the idea that I always mess up even come from? Having recognised that the label is incorrect, you know if it comes up again to ignore the thought.

Choosing a character for your inner nurturer can also be helpful. It might be a particularly loving family member or a friend who is caring and supportive. This can also be a fictional character. Maybe Sméagol (the good side of Gollum) or Elle Woods in Legally Blonde or the girls in Bridesmaids!

5. Look for the good in yourself.

Every day, we tend to dismiss or not notice the loving and positive behaviours we show. Either because we assume anyone would do them or because we are caught up in the thinking in our heads (quite often our inner critic).

Start to recognise the good in yourself and give them labels. For example, "I put in a lot of effort" or "I listened" or "I had a good idea". Noticing these traits will help you to accept that in your core you are a decent and Good Enough person.

Client Story: Jenny

Jenny has a very successful business, consulting on scientific projects and she employs several other professionals. Although she was very proud of what she has created, Jenny believed she was constantly putting others first and never felt quite Good Enough.

She told me all about the inner critical voice that hounded her every day with negative comments like, "Ooh you shouldn't have done that, they will see that you aren't clever enough" or, "the email they sent was a bit short, I bet they are annoyed with you". And it wasn't just about work, with friends and family her inner critic would pop up with, "You can't drop out of going to see X they will be angry, don't be so lazy".

I identified that Jenny's inner critical voice was a combination of The Underminer and The Conformist, and she recognised the voice as that of an essential person in her early years. Even the tone and words used were the same as this person.

Jenny understood from an intellectual point of view that these were thoughts and could not harm her. But she had not yet seen for herself that this was true. I asked her to record situations where her inner critic showed up and what it said. We then challenged the truth of its words and examples of when it was not, or when she couldn't know if it was true or not.

For example; when she sent an email and her negative voice popped up with, "What if they think you are critical, they won't like you very much?' There is no way Jenny could know what their reaction was or control it, and when she'd sent emails like that to other companies, they had been fine.

Jenny learnt to stop reacting to these judgements by her inner critic and recognised that as Deepak Chopra said:

"What other people think of you is not your business. If you start to make that business your business, you will be offended for the rest of your life."

At the end of her programme, I asked Jenny what she felt about her inner critic now. She replied, "Sometimes I realise it is my made-up thinking, and sometimes I take it seriously, but overall, I give it a lot less importance."
We can't ask for a much better state of mind than that, as it is innate in us as humans to at times be connected with our golden nugget of self-worth and at other times to be caught up in our thinking.

Self-Coaching Activity

1. Which of the seven types of inner critic do you identify with?

2. Start to take notice of when your negative voice pops up, what is the situation, what is it saying and who does it sound like?

3. Have a go at drawing what your inner critic looks like, with a speech bubble saying the negative words you have heard. Even if you are not a great artist, this can be fun and another step to de-personalising your inner critic.

4. Reflect on your inner nurturer, what are the words and emotions they share with you? Imagine their voice supporting you.

In A Nutshell

- We have two different voices inside us, an inner critic and an inner nurturer. Unfortunately for many of us, the inner critic is louder and stronger than the nurturer.
- There are seven different types of inner critic:
  - The Perfectionist
  - The Inner Controller
  - The Taskmaster
  - The Underminer
  - The Destroyer
  - The Guilt Tripper
  - The Conformist
- By recognising the critical voice, challenging it and depersonalising it, you can rebalance the weight of the inner critic versus the inner nurturer.
- Most importantly remember that your inner critic is just a thought, with no power or control over you.

Chapter 4

The Danger of Perfectionism

"Don't aim for perfection. Aim for 'better than yesterday'."
Izey Victoria Odiase

Are you someone who works really hard to ensure every detail on a project is 'right'? Do you hate making a mistake and see it as a failure? Maybe you procrastinate about starting a task in case it's too difficult, and you can't do it perfectly?

These are typical behaviours of someone with perfectionism, but what do we mean by the term perfectionism?

In psychological terms, perfectionism is described as a personality trait characterised by the person striving for flawlessness and setting high-performance standards along with being highly self-critical and concerned at other people's opinion of them.

In my experience of working with many clients who have perfectionist traits, a number of them say, "I can't be a perfectionist, because nothing in my life is perfect" but it isn't about things being perfect; it's about thinking things *need* to be perfect and continually pursuing it.

That means rather than accepting you are okay as you are, and connecting with your golden nugget of self-worth, a perfectionist will be on a continual treadmill chasing the elusive feeling of having everything in their lives be 'right'.

Perfectionism is on the increase, and the millennial generation is particularly struggling with high expectations. The rise in the number of perfectionists was identified in research by Thomas Curran of Bath University and Andrew Hill of York University in their study *Perfectionism is Increasing Over Time*.[ix]

They concluded that perfectionism is increasing and the reason for that they suggest is that young people now face more competitive environments, unrealistic expectations and more anxious and controlling parents than generations before.

This is worrying because perfectionism can come hand in hand with depression, anxiety and obsessive-compulsive disorder.

While you may feel that having high standards has driven your career and helped you create exceptional work, in the long term, it may be sabotaging your progress, causing you to procrastinate and be less effective.

As I said in chapter one, looking outside of yourself to find things that will make you feel Good Enough is focusing in the wrong direction. No amount of career success or validation from others is going to give you the 'okayness' you are looking for.

When you do briefly achieve your high expectations and get the feeling that things are 'right' in your life, it is only temporary, and you will move onto the next achievement or whatever you feel will mean that you are Good Enough.

Rather than focusing on feeling acceptable from the outside in, turn your attention to the inside out. Your reality is a result of the thoughts and feelings that you project onto life, rather than the messages and reactions you receive from the outside.

How do I know if I'm a perfectionist?

There are three types of perfectionistic behaviour as described by Hewitt and Flett (1991)[x]. They are:

1. **Self-Oriented perfectionism**. As the name suggests, in this behaviour, the focus is on you being perfect. That means having extremely high expectations of yourself and what you achieve. By setting these unrealistic goals, you are setting yourself up to fail as no one can repeatedly meet perfection (whatever perfection is).

2. **Socially Prescribed perfectionism**. This second type of perfectionism means you feel like society demands very high standards of you, that other people are judging you harshly, and you need to be perfect to gain their approval.

3. **Other-Oriented perfectionism**. When you have high standards of yourself, it can lead to expecting perfection of others and being hard on them when they don't meet your perceived standards.

> *In general, people who display these perfectionist behaviours are trying to hide the fact that they feel insecure and inadequate in some way. They believe that other people are better than them, and to be equal, they need to be flawless.*

Can you imagine how it would be if you were perfect? Other people would probably find you very annoying as you would reflect their shortcomings. I can't believe you would be much fun either, as aren't the stories we tell about our mistakes and failures very entertaining?

If I raise the idea that a client may be a perfectionist with them, many will agree immediately, and others will say they don't aim for perfection, just very high standards.

To me, there is no difference. If your standards are unrealistically high and impossible for a human being with all their innate flaws to continually achieve, then you are a perfectionist.

The typical behaviours of a perfectionist

These are the most common signs of perfectionism I regularly see in my clients and may be true for you:

- Do you expect very high standards for yourself and others? If you are spending too much time on the work you deliver and if you stress about whether it's

Good Enough, then your expectations may be too high.

- When you achieve success against these standards, it only gives you a temporary feeling of satisfaction. You then move on to the next challenge without acknowledging or celebrating your success.

- If you don't achieve the high standards or goals you have set, then you will be very hard on yourself, beating yourself up for even the smallest mistake for a long time.

- Your thinking is all or nothing. That means that for you, something is either 100% right or it's a failure. There is no grey area in between for Good Enough.

- You find it hard to delegate work because others do not complete it to your standards, which means it's just easier to do it yourself. That also allows you to feel in control of the outcome.

- Are you a procrastinator? If so, you will find it challenging to get started on projects and put off beginning work by distracting yourself with other activities. Delaying starting means you can't fail or deliver work that in your perception, is not Good Enough.

- Are rules a big part of your life and is the word 'should' a frequent phrase in your internal vocabulary? The pressure you put on yourself to stick to these rules can make life very tough

- You find yourself analysing and ruminating on situations that haven't gone as well as you wanted or overthinking 'what if' worries in the future.

- You have constant anxiety about what you need to get done

Are you a healthy or neurotic perfectionist?

In the blog *'How to Overcome Perfectionism: Your Complete Guide'*, Celestine Chua discusses the behaviours associated with a healthy perfectionism in contrast to those of neurotic perfectionism.

Use the table below to assess which category you fall into.

How do you overcome these perfectionist traits?

	Healthy Perfectionism	Neurotic Perfectionism
1. Relationship with goals	You feel positively motivated by your goals. There's a sense of excitement, joy as you work on them.	You often feel weighed down by your goals. There's a sense of fear that you may not succeed or do as well as you like.
2. Bias for action	You focus on taking action, while improving as you go along	You constantly procrastinate, in anticipation of that "perfect" moment to do something
3. Personal Satisfaction	You celebrate every small victory and give yourself credit where credit is due	You feel constant dissatisfaction with what you've created or achieved, always feeling that nothing is ever "enough"
4. Macro vs. Micro	You recognize the big picture and do what is necessary to achieve the best outcome, never getting caught up with little details	You obsess about correcting tiny mistakes (that have no impact on the big picture), often at the expense of other priorities
5. Work vs. Self	You have a healthy focus on personal health, relationships, and rest	You constantly neglect your personal health, relationships, and rest time for work
6. Attitude toward failures	When failures happen, you focus on learning from them. You understand failure is part and parcel of success.	You hate failure. You beat yourself up over every failure, even small mistakes.
7. Attitude toward the past mistakes	You use past mistakes as positive learning points to be better	You feel regret over things that are long past

© Celestine Chua, Learn to overcome perfectionism: http://personalexcellence.co/blog/perfectionism/

I would call myself a recovering perfectionist. I spent most of my corporate career not realising I had perfectionist traits, and most of my coaching career challenging and being curious about those behaviours.

My perfectionism comes from a mixture of upbringing and the fact that I love learning and developing and being the best I can. In my childhood, I was conditioned to believe that only excellence gets rewarded and to link that reward to love and security.

I wasn't a typical perfectionist in that my room has never been meticulously tidy, and I'm not focused on every detail being correct. I do, though, have very high standards for myself and others and a very competitive streak in my nature.

I remember even in my primary school days I wasn't competing with myself to improve my skills. Instead, I would judge myself entirely on how I did in comparison to others.

One of my natural abilities at school was being good at maths. In my class, there was also another boy who excelled in the subject and always scored slightly higher than me. I pushed myself to improve so I could beat him in a test, and when I did, there was a momentary feeling of, 'Yay!' particularly when the teacher praised me. It was then followed by thinking, 'Yes, but you are not as good at X, Y and Z as he is' and I was back in that anxious thought cycle.

Overthinking and ruminating were another of my unhelpful thought patterns. I still find myself having the memory of a bad situation triggered occasionally. It always fills me with a feeling of shame. I know that in my mind, I have exaggerated the situation and that ruminating on it only hurts. I can now disrupt my thinking to not jump into the memory.

The successful strategies that my clients and I have used to let go of aspects of perfectionism are a combination of mindset shifts and practical steps. I'll share a few with you below:

Ask Yourself, 'What is perfectionism costing me?'

Reflecting on how perfectionism might be harming your emotions, your health and other people is a good motivator for you to change. For example:

1. Is it causing you to feel stressed and anxious?
2. Is your partner fed up that you spend more time working than with them?

A friend of mine described himself as a workaholic. He was also a perfectionist, which led to him working very long hours. David's fear of not being Good Enough or of making a mistake drove him to expect impossibly high standards of himself. Like most of us, his 'to do' list at work never came to an end, there was always more work waiting.

As you can imagine, working evenings and weekends on top of regular hours wasn't sustainable for him. It affected his mental health, his marriage and his bond with their children.

It took a series of scary panic attacks to wake David up to the fact that he was dispensable and there was a limit to the amount and the quality of work he could deliver. He now has strict boundaries on his working hours and is working on setting realistic expectations.

Make sure your expectations are realistic

One of the biggest obstacles a perfectionist has is that their expectations of themselves are impossibly high. To help with this, every time you start a new project, report or presentation, challenge yourself to check if your standards are achievable. If you were to spend 10 or 20% less time on them, would they be Good Enough?

Lowering your standards can feel uncomfortable, so I suggest you do it a small step at a time.

A common worry about lowering your expectations is that you'll have no standards or perform poorly. In fact, realistic standards allow you to do your best without cost to your health and relationships.

Julie was a perfectionist who believed she needed to have tight control over her department and their work. She would spend days collating and checking over the data and detail in her monthly report for the senior team. The report was well known in the company for being a gold-plated, high standard commentary.

However, Julie was always short of time, stressed and worried that she couldn't keep up with the expectations she'd created of her work.

I challenged her to spend only one day and not four days on the report. She found this suggestion worrying but agreed to do it.

In the end, she spent about a day and a half and produced what was in her mind an unfinished overview. The interesting consequence was that she got no feedback about her brief report. It turned out that none of the senior managers ever read all the detail she sent anyway!

Julie has now not only continued with the brief reports but has also delegated it to a team member and is loving the extra time to focus on her projects.

Face your fears

Worrying that they will make a mistake and be judged harshly for it is one of the greatest fears of a perfectionist. As with any phobia, a gradual exposure to that fear can build up your tolerance.

As I described with Julie above, testing out what happens when you don't achieve your very high expectations can lead to new freedom.

Challenge yourself to do something that you naturally wouldn't do, such as:

3. Arrive 10 minutes late for a meeting
4. Speak up in a meeting without having rehearsed what you want to say or knowing if it's right

5. Send your emails without double and triple checking them for mistakes
6. Go out to work without tidying the kitchen

Perfectionists tend to catastrophise the outcomes of anything imperfect. As a pharmacist, if I made an error with medication, then the result could be a catastrophe for the patient. Many jobs have that possibility of harming others or losing significant amounts of money and it's important to be aware of potential risks and to mitigate for them. However, constantly going down the 'what if' worry spiral and overthinking every situation is likely to make you less effective as well as highly stressed.

Rarely does this type of worrying lead you to an effective plan or a solution. It's when your mind is quieter that your 'Eureka' moments pop up.

The strategy of deliberately being imperfect, in an appropriate situation, helps you to recognise that not being perfect isn't a catastrophe and that being imperfect is just being human.

Be Present

Being truly present in the moment stops us from being distracted by thoughts about what we 'should' be doing or ruminating on a mistake we've made. Whether it's out on a dog walk, watching a football match or listening to music, the feeling of being present can empty your mind.

Unfortunately, perfectionism is the opposite of this. It keeps you up in your mind with anxious thoughts spinning and bringing with them uncomfortable feelings. An antidote to this anxious thinking is to be present or in the 'flow' (being so absorbed in something that time passes without you realising).

When do you feel the most present or in flow?

How can you bring more of that feeling into your life?

Aim for Excellence

Rather than trying to be perfect, strive for excellence instead. Excellence is a value rather than a personality trait like perfectionism and is something you may have in your core values or something you can develop.

The definition of excellence is being outstanding or extremely good, and you can achieve it by using these ideas:

1. **Focus on the good**. Every career or part of life has aspects you won't enjoy. Look for the positives and focus on solutions rather than problems.

2. **Be curious**. A mindset of curiosity rather than negativity will bring out the best in you and others. If a colleague behaves badly, be curious as to why rather than taking it personally.

3. **Take a risk**. To be successful, you are going to need to risk failure, and like a lot of motivational quotes say, you can learn more from failure than any success.

4. **Commit to hard work**. Excellence doesn't come easily, but as a perfectionist, I'm sure hard work doesn't scare you. Being passionate about your career or activity helps to maintain motivation.

5. **Challenge yourself to grow**. This doesn't mean setting unrealistic standards, but instead acknowledging your successes and then moving onto another challenge.

When you're working towards excellence, you'll feel in touch with your intuition. If you've fallen into perfectionism, you may feel frustration, irritability and fear. Remember perfectionism is a game you can't win.

Client story: Kay

Kay was a classic perfectionist; she worked incredibly long hours in her management consultant role and travelled abroad a lot. Being single, she felt this was expected of her, and she would sacrifice her social life and 'me time' to get ahead in her career.

She contacted me when she was due to return to work after a month off with a stress-related illness. Kay wanted to focus on putting boundaries in place around her working hours and to find a way of reducing the stress levels she felt in her role.

Through our coaching sessions, I got a clear picture of Kay at work. Her bosses gave her great feedback, but it washed over her head as she over-analysed anything that she deemed negative. She judged both herself, her peers and her seniors harshly, at the same time as using their strengths as a stick to drive her perfectionism.

Interestingly, Kay regularly felt the organisation undervalued her and that she wasn't receiving the support and progression she deserved. This resentment at the company not meeting her high expectations added to her perfectionist 'all or nothing' thinking, led to her repeatedly talking about resigning.

You might say that she was an ambitious and driven woman and that there is nothing wrong with that. I would agree with you, except for the fact that she was unhappy, stressed and having little life outside of work.

It took a while for Kay to see how her mindset and expectations were working against her. Then she realised that the reason she worked so hard was that she wanted to have a career that made her feel Good Enough. Her understanding then shifted, and we worked practically on how she could put boundaries in place to protect her emotional and physical health.

Kay also applied the 80/20 rule – where 80% of the work is done by 20% of the effort and only if you put in another 80% of energy will you achieve the remaining 20% of perfection. Seeing her expectations as a guide to what she wanted to achieve rather than an absolute, enabled her to lift her head out of all the detail.

The most significant shift for Kay was accepting that her career didn't define her value. She was Good Enough whatever job she had, whatever salary she earned, and whether she was top or bottom of the business development table. This meant that she was still ambitious and driven, but knowing at her core her self-worth was in tact it felt less stressful.

Self-Coaching Activity

Perfectionism is all about wanting things to feel perfect. If your perfectionism is unhealthy, consider these self-coaching activities:

1. **Reflect on the expectations** you have about your work, social life, physical appearance etc. Are they realistic? What would Good Enough in those areas of your life look like?
2. **Focus on your positives**. Keep a journal and every night or every few days detail three things you are doing right, have achieved or are proud of. Keeping your focus away from what you haven't met or what you aren't perfect at is helpful.
3. **Stop judging others**. When you purposely stop yourself judging others, you'll find that it will also affect your judgements on yourself. Be aware of when you are doing it and refocus your thinking.

In A Nutshell

- Perfectionism isn't about everything being perfect, it's about thinking things *need* to be perfect and continually pursuing it.

- Challenge your expectations. Are they realistic? Would you expect others to achieve them? What is having these expectations costing you?
- Looking outside of yourself in order to find things that will make you feel Good Enough is focusing in the wrong direction.
- Facing your fears by deliberately being imperfect is the right place to start in overcoming your perfectionism.
- Strive for excellence rather than perfection.

Chapter 5

Tackling the Imposter

"Imposter Syndrome is the province of the successful, of the high-achievers, of the perfectionists. That's the irony."
Kate Hilton

What is this term Imposter Syndrome? It's what a lot of women think is the reason they lack confidence; does it have a real definition?

> *Psychologists define Imposter Syndrome as, 'A collection of feelings of inadequacy that persist despite evident success.'*

In other words, you feel that you are not Good Enough despite all the success you have achieved.

When I ask my clients about their achievements and successes in their career, a lot of them struggle to come up with ten. I then remind them of the accomplishments we've discussed, and I'll get responses like, "Oh yes, I was really lucky to get that role, I don't think they had many applicants" or, "That was no big deal, anyone could have done it". Even, "That isn't an achievement, it was far too easy."

My 'favourite' comment was, "I'm the only woman in the senior team and I know I'm only there for diversity, so I don't speak up". How scary is it that such amazing women don't see their successes?

Imposter Syndrome isn't only characterised by refusing to claim credit for your achievements. It is also how you react to the smallest of flaws or mistakes. Do you ruminate over them and give yourself a tough time?

For example, if you submitted a report which you knew was only 99% perfect and no one spotted the missing 1%, would you feel you got away with it?

Imposter Syndrome is not an actual disorder but a description of the behaviours of people who have internalised fear of being exposed as a fraud. It was clinical psychologists Pauline Clance and Suzanne Imes[xi] who first gave it the name Imposter Syndrome in 1978.

> *Research has suggested that at least 70% of people have struggled with Imposter Syndrome in their career or life. Despite the initial belief that it was primarily in high achieving women, it is equally an issue for men and women.*

Recent research by NatWest as part of its #OwnYourImposter campaign[xii], found that 28% of working women feel like Imposter Syndrome has stopped them speaking in a meeting. It also found 21% have been prevented from suggesting a new or alternative idea at work, and 26% have failed to change career or role.

Many famous people have openly said they struggle with Imposter Syndrome. Emma Watson, David Bowie, Maya Angelou, Lady Gaga have all publicly said they struggle with it. Even Tom Hanks once said, "No matter what we've done, there comes a point where you think, 'How did I get here? When are they going to discover that I am, in fact, a fraud and take everything away from me?'"

Sheryl Sandberg in her book *Lean In – Women, Work and the Will To Lead,* said, "… many people, but especially women, feel fraudulent when they are praised for their accomplishments. Instead of feeling worthy of recognition, they feel undeserving and guilty, as if a mistake has been made. Despite being high achievers, even experts in their fields, women can't seem to shake the sense that it is only a matter of time until they are found out for who they really are - impostors with limited skills or abilities."

I've heard famous fellow coach Michael Neill[xiii], tell the story of working with one of the richest men in the country. This man had a fear that the money he'd earned was just by luck and that he would wake up one morning having lost all his money and everyone would know he was a fraud.

If someone that rich could still be anxious about being an imposter, doesn't it suggest that money makes no difference when you don't believe in yourself?

Imposter Syndrome occurs in reaction to specific circumstances. You may be very comfortable presenting to a group of peers but be full of self-doubt when you have to speak at a conference of strangers. Perhaps you find small talk at networking events torture, but at a social event with new people you are relaxed.

There are common characteristics that make you more likely to suffer from Imposter Syndrome. These are: perfectionism, fear of failure, 'nice girl' conditioning, previous bullying and dominating parents. Imposter Syndrome, as with perfectionism in the last chapter, is also linked to anxiety and depression.

Do you struggle with Imposter Syndrome?

Complete the questionnaire to see if Imposter Syndrome is an issue for you.

Do you...	Yes	No
Ever feel like a fraud in any part of your life?		
Ever feel that others don't see you truly as you are?		
Believe that if they saw you deep down, they might not like what they saw?		
Ever feel as though you don't fit in?		
Take longer than others to prepare for a meeting or presentation?		

Feel like a failure if you make a mistake?		
Have a hard time asking for help because you think you should know how to do it? Feel upset when you receive feedback that you perceive as negative?		
Feel you need to make things perfect all the time?		
Think your successes are external to you?		

What does your score mean?

0-2 Yes. Imposter Syndrome is not an issue for you – it's unlikely to be affecting your performance and self-esteem.

3-5 Yes. You probably experience Imposter Syndrome but only occasionally and although it may make you doubt yourself sometimes it doesn't have much effect on your performance.

6-8 Yes. You experience the Imposter Syndrome frequently and intensely. It will be affecting your confidence and holding you back from the success you deserve.

8-10 Yes. The Imposter Syndrome will be derailing your performance most of the time. This mindset will limit your ability to succeed. Addressing it will free you to demonstrate your real potential.

Dr Valerie Young [xiv] is an expert in the Imposter Syndrome and has spent the last forty years helping people who suffer from it. She believes that imposters have a distorted view of what being competent means, and until they challenge this, they will continue to lack confidence and feel like a fraud.

In her book *The Secret Thoughts of Successful Women: Why Capable People Suffer From the Imposter Syndrome and How to Thrive in Spite of It* [xv], Valerie describes using an exercise called *What's In Your Rule Book?* in her workshops. She asks the attendees to complete the following sentence:

If I was intelligent, capable and competent...

Whoever the people on the workshop are and whatever their background, the same kind of responses come up. The most common being:

If I was intelligent, capable and competent, I'd...

- Know everything in my field

- Get it right the first time

- Excel in everything I do

- Always know the answer

- Always understand what I'm reading

- Always feel confident

- Never make a mistake

- Never be confused

- Never need help

When you read it like that, doesn't it sound ridiculous? Who would ever expect anyone to perform at this level?

Hopefully, you can now see that imposters have a crazy idea of what competence means and if you are judging yourself that way, it is time for a rethink.

Valerie's research on these internal rules that imposters show led her to categorise them into five different types[xvi]. Do any of them sound like you?

The 5 Types of Imposter Syndrome

1. **The Perfectionist.** Success for a perfectionist can be unsatisfying as they believe they could have done better and will be found out as being a fraud. Their focus is on the 'how' work is done and 'how' it turns out. When they have achieved success, they move on to the next challenge without acknowledging their achievement.

   Tip - As a perfectionist, you can help yourself by starting to listen to your internal validation rather than relying on the approval of others.

2. **The Natural Genius.** This type of imposter not only has high standards but also believes they need to have the ability to achieve something the first time and smoothly.

A Natural Genius might have a track record of excelling and achieving things with little effort and being known as the 'clever' one. As a result, they expect to do everything quickly, and when they don't, it can knock their confidence. Making them feel they are not Good Enough for their job.

Tip - Recognising that some skills need to be developed, can overcome these beliefs. Challenge yourself to be a work in progress on behaviours that don't come naturally and accept that this is okay.

3. **The Soloist.** If you are a Soloist, then you hate to ask for help and believe that you should be able to achieve things by yourself. The Soloist cares most about 'who' completes the task.

    If they can't complete the task on their own, then it is a sign of failure.

    Tip - it's okay to do things independently, but you also need to recognise that making use of other resources doesn't affect your worth or value in the job.

4. **Superwoman.** This imposter is a workaholic and multitasker. They define their worth on 'how many' roles or tasks they can balance and deliver. These may include: parent, wife, daughter, colleague, boss, friend, volunteer and many more.

They enjoy the validation they get from others who say, "I don't know how you do it all". They work harder and harder to achieve their idea of what good looks like. It is a need to hide their flaws and insecurities that drives them to work so hard, and they feel they didn't deserve or earn their position and thus need to prove themselves.

Tip - If this sounds like you, are you addicted to working itself, rather than to the work? Put some boundaries in place to the hours you work and focus on validating yourself internally rather than looking for external approval. If you don't do this, you may find that relationships, hobbies and friends all suffer.

5. **The Expert.** The Expert is a knowledge version of the perfectionist, and their focus is on 'what' and 'how much' they know. If they have even a small lack of knowledge, they feel like a failure and an imposter.

    Being in a situation where others have more knowledge is very uncomfortable for an expert. They are scared that they will never know enough and will get exposed as inexperienced or lacking.

    Logically, I'm sure experts know that you can never know everything, but that doesn't stop them endlessly looking for new information to improve and feel secure. This constant need to know more can result in procrastination, as they spend time trying to soak up all the information they might need before starting on a task.

Tip - to overcome this type of Imposter Syndrome, practise the belief that it's okay to get back to people when you don't have the answer and that using other resources doesn't make you an imposter.

You can also give 'just in time learning' a go, which means acquiring a skill or knowledge only when you need it.

How Do I Stop Feeling Like an Imposter?

As you have probably noticed, there is a lot of overlap between a perfectionist and an imposter, the biggest being that imposters, like perfectionists, have lost their connection with that golden nugget of self-worth. They are seeing their value only in what they achieve or what others say about them. That is why the work we did in chapter one, 'Why Aren't I Good Enough?' is so important.

The strategies I mentioned in the previous chapter of recognising the cost of perfectionism, facing your fears and being present will all help you to overcome your imposter. Other strategies to consider are:

1. **Speak to someone you trust**. Being able to talk about the worry that you are a fraud with someone who understands and doesn't judge you can be the first step to changing your mindset. Imposter Syndrome might be something people have heard of,

but very few men and women are comfortable to admit to it. You can change that.

Despite the new openness around mental health issues that have developed over the last few years, people still feel discomfort in talking about what is happening in their mind, in case it is seen as weakness.

My clients are very honest and open with me but are often surprised to hear that so many other women are having the same thoughts as them. We tend to hide our insecurities behind a mask of confidence that stops us sharing our real feelings.

If you don't have people in your life who you are happy to discuss this with, then you could find a mentor at work, work with a professional such as a coach or look for a community online.

2. **Rationalise and reframe it**. Start by identifying your ideas around what being intelligent, capable and competent means. When you challenge those ideas rationally, and with logic, you will, hopefully, recognise that your thoughts are unrealistic.

Seeing that those thoughts are not valid and that you don't have to believe them, act on them or make decisions to change them, will free their hold on you.

I use various metaphors with clients to help them see that their imposter thoughts have no power over

69

them. Some clients like to imagine those thoughts as a backseat driver who rabbits away in the background but can't actually drive the car. So, even though the voice telling you that you are a fraud sounds and feels real, it has no control over what you do. That means you can ignore it as you would white noise in the background, and it will lose its power.

3. **Recognise any truth**. Having just said that your imposter voice is untrue and to ignore it, I am now going to contradict myself by saying that in some situations your self-doubts might actually be true. Imagine being in a position where you are the only woman in the room or joining an event where everyone knows each other. Then it's natural to feel like an outsider or uncomfortable. The important thing to remember is that this feeling is just about not fitting in and NOT about your abilities or value.

Client Story: Anne

Anne works for a large financial services firm and has had a successful career with them. She worked part-time for many years while her children were young and put her career ambitions on hold.

Her children are now at university, and she has returned to full-time work and is ambitious to progress in her career.

From our initial chat, I could tell that Anne fitted the description of having Imposter Syndrome, something that she had heard of but didn't know what it was.

As we started working together, I recognised that from the five different types of imposter, Anne was a perfectionist, an expert and also superwoman of course!

The role that Anne was in required a focus on detail and a knowledge of a lot of regulations, which suited her perfectionist mindset. She had high expectations of both herself and her team, and the fear that a mistake would be made was a constant worry for her.

The volume of regulations around her work meant that Anne could never know everything, but as an expert, she felt she should. When Anne attended a meeting, she would have spent the weekend or night before cramming on knowledge to avoid the catastrophe of not knowing something.

Her long working hours meant a loss of her 'me-time' and Anne was getting close to burnout. She reached out to me wanting to change her working behaviours and to challenge this feeling of being an imposter.

As Anne said to me afterwards, having the opportunity to explore her feelings around Imposter Syndrome had reduced her sense of shame and guilt about them.

The insight that gave Anne her 'Ahah!' moment was when I told her that the only difference between someone who struggles with Imposter Syndrome and someone who doesn't is the way they think about a situation. A person without Imposter Syndrome is no smarter, more intelligent or competent than you.

Anne has now recognised she doesn't need to take as much notice of her imposter's voice. If she doesn't interact with it, she has a kinder attitude towards herself.

As a result, she is now more of the person she wants to be rather than the person she thinks she 'should' be. This change has led (to Anne's surprise) to more respect and recognition from colleagues and seniors and being told she is ready for promotion.

Self-Coaching Activity

1. Identify the situations when you are aware of your Imposter thoughts. What are the triggers for your self-doubt thinking?
2. Are any of these thoughts true? Could you genuinely be feeling you don't fit in or that you are an outsider?
3. If you believe you should be able to do everything yourself or you should know everything, challenge yourself to ask for help once a day.
4. If you expect to achieve unrealistic high standards in everything, challenge yourself to do something to an 80% Good Enough level.
5. Remember, the only difference between you and someone who does not have Imposter Syndrome is one thought.

In A Nutshell

- Imposter Syndrome is about not believing you are Good Enough despite all your achievements and feedback. It is feeling you are only where you are because of luck, and at some point, others will find out you are a fraud.

- People with Imposter Syndrome have a ridiculously high belief of what competence is.
- Imposter Syndrome has been categorised into five types: the perfectionist, the expert, the soloist, the natural genius and the superwoman.
- Your thoughts about being an imposter are not real, you don't have to believe them or engage with them.
- The difference between someone with Imposter Syndrome and someone without is just a thought.

Chapter 6

Comparititis

"A flower does not think of competing with the flower next to it, it just blooms"
Zen Shin

If you are on social media - and 2.77 Billion of us are - then you have probably had that gut-churning moment when you see a post showing friends or colleagues having a fantastic time.

Perhaps they are on holiday, a night out, doing something charitable or sharing a career success. We have all had that feeling that others are doing, being or looking better than us.

Comparititis, as I like to call it, is the disease of comparing yourself to others and women, in particular, seem to be very susceptible to catching it. We ignore our core self-worth that tells us we're Good Enough and instead focus on external validation.

You have probably heard of the studies that have linked social media use to depression. In 2018, for example, the University of Pennsylvania published a study in the Journal of Social and Clinical Psychology looking at the effects of social media on loneliness, anxiety, fear of missing out (FOMO) and depression[xvii].

74

They tested the effects of reducing social media time to only 30 minutes per day for three weeks, and this demonstrated a significant improvement in well-being, in particular in loneliness and depression.

This scares me for my teenage daughter and son, as we haven't yet seen the effects that this social media culture will play out in later life. Hopefully, the increase in openness around mental health will encourage the new generation to talk about any issues.

Social media isn't the only circumstance where comparisons take place. I know from my own experience that it's possible to make comparisons in almost every situation in life.

Why do we compare ourselves to others?

Comparing ourselves to others is a natural human impulse; our mind is designed to work that way. By watching other humans, it enables us to learn from them whether it was how to hunt food in caveman days, or how to read and write today.

There is even a theory about it, the Social Comparison Theory, which was developed by Leon Festinger in 1954[xviii]. It states that individuals determine their own social and personal worth based on how they compare to others.

As humans, we have an ability to self-reflect, which is why we ponder over our purpose and why we can collaborate and compete with fellow humans.

To do this, we need to be able to evaluate ourselves, and you can only do that if you have another person against which to measure yourself.

Leon Festinger also hypothesised that the more similar we believe a person is to us, the more likely we are to compare ourselves to them. You are less likely to compare yourself to the CEO of your company than to a colleague at your level. Also, when the individual or group is vital to us, we are more likely to make comparisons.

We can use this social comparison in positive ways as well, as discussed by Rebecca Webber in The Comparison Trap[xix]. For example, to grow and motivate ourselves. When you started in your career, you may have looked to experienced or successful people in the same company to evaluate yourself.

> *Positively comparing yourself can support self-improvement and be a powerful tool for career progression.*

In the same way, a downward comparison to someone who is not quite at your level of seniority or ability can give a boost to your self-esteem. For example, if a new join is brought into your team of peers and they have less experience and skill, it will probably give you a temporary lift in confidence.

It is, however, the negative connotations of comparing ourselves to others that most of us choose to overthink. That sharp flash of envy when a colleague gets the praise you were hoping would come your way. The critical voice in your head that tells you that you are not Good Enough when you are passed over for promotion.

Research at Essex and Cambridge University in 2015[xx] discovered that this focus on comparison is highest when we are young and decreases with age. Probably, the study states, because as we get older, we start to compare ourselves to our past rather than to other people.

As a competitive person and academically bright, I compared myself a lot at school, in what I think (looking back) was a positive way. It wasn't until I went to university and was thrown in with an overwhelming number of different types of people that I remember the negative thoughts beginning.

I think it was a need to fit in with my new friends and fellow students that was behind my self-doubts. I would find myself comparing everything about other students, from how attractive they were, how fashionable, how bright, how chatty, how many friends and boyfriends.

The majority of my comparisons were upward, but in a way that was detrimental to me. For the first time in my life, I worried about my weight and how many friends I had. Why was I doing this? Partly to benchmark myself against others and understand where I fitted in (on my own made up scale), and partly to feel better about me. I was obsessively making comparisons to boost my self-esteem, but it was backfiring. Instead of being positive, it was unhealthy and toxic, leaving me with lower self-esteem and confidence. I had no idea then that my golden nugget of self-worth existed and that I was okay without having to compare to others.

What I have now realised, is that I wasn't even comparing my real self to others, I was evaluating what I believed about myself instead.

If you believe that you are terrible at presentations, when a colleague presents successfully, you compare their abilities to your belief about you, and not the real you. As you can imagine, that means you assess yourself as not being Good Enough, and that affects your self-esteem and can leave you feeling miserable.

When we have these uncomfortable feelings, to make ourselves feel better, we end up tearing the other person down, either internally in our mind or by offloading to others. Again, we might get a temporary boost from this, but it is not long before those uncomfortable feelings return.

What does all this mean for you?

It means that comparing yourself to others is wired into our brains, and it is not something we can turn off. The good news is that as you can differentiate 'evaluation' comparisons and 'feel better' comparisons, you can stop doing the negative type and feel motivated by the evaluation comparison instead.

Become aware of when you are making comparisons, you can then ask yourself, "Why am I doing this? Is it to assess my skill or behaviour or to make myself feel better?"

If it is the second, then, recognise that this behaviour is unhealthy and refocus your mind.

The reality is that you are not even comparing apples with apples because you are seeing the window dressing of the other person. The outside image that they want you to see, on social media or face to face. You are comparing that with the whole of you, flaws and insecurities included.

Does that sound fair?

How do I recover from my comparititis?

As I said above, the first step is to be aware of when you are comparing and identify the triggers and situations where you are prone to doing it.

You can then determine the motivation behind your comparititis. If it is making you miserable, then it's highly likely to be a 'feel better' and ego-based driver.

Logically that should be enough to stop us doing this self-sabotaging behaviour, but as I said, evaluation and comparing are an intrinsic part of being human.

My clients find it helpful to focus their comparititis only on themselves, rather than on someone you can never fully evaluate.

I ask them to think about the following questions:

1. **What things do I usually compare myself to others on**? These ideas could be the speed of your career progression, your relationship with your boss, your popularity, work ethic, expertise or presentation skills etc.
2. **Where were you in your career 1 to 5 years ago**? Score yourself out of ten as to how well you were doing on the things you listed for question one, with

five being I was doing okay but needed to develop and ten being I was awesome!

3. **Now score yourself on the same areas today**. Have your scores improved? If yes, great and how else can you develop them further to move up another number? If no, then what was the reason for that, and what would a realistic target be instead?

The purpose of this is to help you look at developing yourself in comparison to your *past self* rather than to others.

> *Remember that life is a journey, and we all have our own route. It is not about where you rank on that journey, what you have achieved or own compared to others. Instead, it's about what you want to do and the direction you want to go. There is no right or wrong way for your journey to pan out, enjoy the view.*

Client Story – Hannah

Hannah felt the company she worked for were treating her unfairly and she described this during our first discussion. She is an accountant in a small industrial company, and despite putting in long hours, being loyal and delivering well, she felt they weren't valuing her.

Hannah talked me through many instances of how her boss never listened to her ideas, she wasn't given the same opportunities her colleagues were and that she'd done nothing to deserve this behaviour.

If you have ever heard of the victim mindset, then you'll understand this is what Hannah was displaying. It is a personality trait in which people tend to see themselves as victims of the negative actions of others, even if there is evidence to disprove it.

Hannah's descriptions of her colleague's behaviour showed me that she had compared herself to them and was feeling very uncomfortable with the results. To feel better about herself, she was attacking her boss and colleagues in her mind and seeing herself as being mistreated.

It took Hannah a while to see that by placing all the responsibility for the situations on the other person, she was putting herself into victim mode. When she saw that she needed to look at her role and take responsibility for her actions, she began to move forward.

We then started to explore the comparisons she was making between herself and her colleagues and the effect that was having on her mindset. The two areas that Hannah frequently compared herself to others on were the influence they had on decisions made by their boss and popularity in the office.

As Hannah began to realise that these comparisons were making her miserable, she decided to think about how she could work on improving her impact and influence, rather than resenting the skills of the others.

By the end of our programme, Hannah's motivation at work and enjoyment of the role had improved. She felt valued by her boss and confident in her capabilities. Her relationships in the office hadn't developed as much as she would have liked, but she was pragmatic about it and not blaming others.

She's since moved company and is blossoming in her new role with a new team.

Self-Coaching Activity

1. Become aware of when you are comparing yourself to others and what is motivating you. Is it to know where you are so you can develop or is it a need to feel better about yourself?
2. If it is to boost your self-esteem, then keep the focus on your development using my exercise above to score your progress. Recognise your own successes and how fabulous you are rather than looking at others.
3. What does career success mean to you? Do you want to be an executive, to move up to the next role, to work for yourself or are you happy where you are if you felt Good Enough? Knowing the direction of your journey helps you to see that others are on a different route, so comparing is unhelpful.
4. Who do you admire and respect in your company or industry? Think about what it is that they do that you appreciate. Use them as a motivation for your self-growth.

In A Nutshell

- We are wired to compare ourselves to others, but when we do it to feel better, it becomes harmful and knocks our self-esteem.
- Social media has driven an increase in people struggling with comparititis.

- When you compare yourself to others, you are comparing your idea of you, flaws and all, with the best version of them.
- Be aware of whether you are comparing to genuinely benchmark yourself against another person or just to give your self-esteem a boost.
- Focus on your own improvement as a comparison and not on other people

Chapter 7

Keeping the Power

"It took me quite a long time to develop a voice, and now that I have it, I am not going to be silent."
Madeleine K. Albright

What do I mean by 'keeping your power'?

Have you ever been in a meeting with people of mixed seniorities, there is a lively discussion going on, and you want to be part of the debate but are struggling to find something to say? By the time you are ready, either someone else has already mentioned it, or the conversation has moved on?

Or, have you ever had an opinion or idea you wanted to share, but found it difficult to speak up in case it isn't the 'right' answer?

If that sounds like you, then I'm afraid you are giving away your power.

When anyone is invited to attend a meeting, presentation or one to one, they bring with them a power to contribute to the discussion. That power means you have as much right as any other person there to give your thoughts and opinions, regardless of pay packet or job title. It doesn't mean your idea has the same weight as, for example, the CEO, but you do have the same right to share.

When you hold yourself back from speaking, you are giving away that power, and it often goes to the loudest person in the room.

Imagine that power is a bright light, and when you enter the room, you are all carrying one of these beams (think Jedi). As the meeting begins and you all introduce yourself, everyone's light is burning with the same brightness. After ten minutes when you haven't spoken, your light starts to dim. After twenty minutes you notice that the light of the most talkative person is shining brighter and yours is even dimmer. You can feel yourself becoming difficult to see.

By the end of the meeting, you are entirely in shadow, yet other contributors are blazing with light. You have given your power away, and as a result, others are shining.

In that scenario, there is probably one person who wants to make sure they are heard and ends up talking for talking's sake. I am not suggesting this approach, and that doesn't necessarily make your light the brightest. But, notice how by not keeping your power, you have put yourself in the shadows.

In 2012 Brigham Young University [xxi]produced a report on a study of 94 groups of mixed men and women. They found that the amount of contribution by males and females was dramatically different. Women spoke for less than 75% of the time that men did, and the more outnumbered the women were by men, the less they spoke.

Interestingly, the writer of the report Karpowitz said, "When women participated more, they brought unique and helpful perspectives to the issue under discussion."

He also added that, "We're not just losing the voice of someone who would say the same things as everybody else in the conversation."

That is a critical point, by not speaking up with your unique voice, not only are you giving away your power, but they don't hear your perspective on the discussion.

Why don't women speak up?

I clearly remember one meeting where, along with a colleague, I was presenting an update on a project to the senior executive. I was nervous, partly because I wanted to make a good impression and secondly as I was worried about saying the wrong thing. The short presentation went okay as we were well prepared. It wasn't until the discussion began and they started asking questions that my nerves about looking stupid kicked in.

My body thought I was in a life-threatening situation and immediately flooded me with adrenaline, known as the fight or flight response. The adrenaline boost made my face flush, and my mind was full of racing thoughts, none of which I felt confident enough to say.

Fortunately, my calm colleague was able to handle the debate, and once my body's panic response was over, I realised things were going well. When I reflected afterwards, I knew that even if no one had noticed my flushing, they would have seen me like a sidekick to my colleague.

That difficult moment gave me the insight that rather than trying to be this slick, articulate and perfect person, I needed to be authentic and comfortable with what I know and believe.

Feeling okay about being yourself is precisely the work I do with my clients. In just a few months, they have a change of mindset around their self-belief and being visible.

> *This fear of saying the wrong thing or looking stupid is a paramount concern of people that struggle to speak up, and it's a belief held more strongly by women than men.*

What is holding women back?

In my research and working with thousands of clients, I believe the main reason behind women's discomfort at speaking up is a combination of lower confidence, being risk-averse and a fear of making a mistake. Add to this all the mindsets we have talked about before such as Imposter Syndrome, Perfectionism, 'Nice Girl' conditioning and workplace culture. It feels a bit scary, doesn't it?

However, I still see a large number of women who have dared to start speaking up, be heard and keep their power. The same can be true for you.

The shared beliefs that hold back the women I have worked with are:

I don't want to say the wrong thing or appear stupid

I have nothing to add of value

I should be respectful to my seniors, and their opinion is more important than mine

I don't have as much knowledge or experience as them; I should listen

I can't disagree with others as they may get upset

I always get interrupted or ignored, so what is the point?

I am a reflective thinker and don't come up with ideas in time

I don't want to appear to talk too much in case I get judged as being loud or aggressive

Do any of these resonate with you, or do you have a different belief that is stopping you from keeping your power?

How do I get the courage to speak up?

Keeping quiet in meetings or discussions can become a habit. When you start a new job, you may think, 'I'll stay quiet to observe and absorb the dynamics'. If you don't begin asking questions and giving your opinion, it becomes habitual behaviour. You become unused to hearing your voice in the meeting. When you then decide you have value to add, it feels uncomfortable, and leads to you being dismissed or interrupted.

Havana Nguyen describes conversations as a ball game in her article *What Happened When I Started Speaking Up in Meetings*[xxii]. I love this metaphor and find it applies to most meetings and one to one discussions.

Depending on the culture, the personalities and the group dynamics, the ball game (discussion) can be:

- Tennis - complete sentences bounce back and forth between people
- Basketball - people spontaneously but naturally picking up the topic as it jumps and shifts around multiple people
- Bowling - people take turns, and everyone gets ample time to plan what they say and complete their sentences
- Rugby - where everyone is clamouring to get their say and sentences get cut off all the time

More often than not, women withhold their comments in a group setting, and end up bowling in a rugby game!

To help you play well at whatever ball game you are in, I've got some crucial strategies for you to try.

1. Preparation

Preparation is essential, especially if you are a reflective thinker. Not only does it give you ideas and questions to contribute, but it also gives your confidence levels a boost knowing you have information prepared.

A lot of women fear that they will say the wrong thing and hold back from speaking up until they are 100% sure their idea is right. If this is you, then having a few ideas you could share in your back pocket can be helpful. Don't research them to see if they are the 'perfect' answer, challenge yourself to contribute one when appropriate without knowing if it's absolutely right. Then as you build self-belief, your confidence in your ideas will build.

2. Set an Intention

I've noticed that a lot of my clients have very high expectations of how they 'should' be behaving and contributing to meetings. The issue with this is it can feel overwhelming and scary, so they don't even get started.

By setting yourself a lower level of intention, you are more likely to achieve it. As you become more comfortable with hearing your voice in these meetings you can raise the challenge level of your intention, making the intention more difficult or complicated, such as sharing an idea as soon as it is in your head rather than waiting until you've thought it through.

When you feel intimidated in a meeting, a straightforward way to start is to ask a question for clarification or to agree with someone else's point. It's important to have spoken in the first 10minutes of a meeting, after that, the pressure of, 'I must speak, I must speak...' can keep you up in your head rather than being part of the discussion. It also ensures that you get the credit for an idea, rather than someone else getting there first!

The next step would be to practise speaking up when your idea is only partially formed. If you overthink your opinion, it can result in procrastinating until the moment has passed.

Another intention could be to challenge a senior person you respect but disagree with, which leads to my point number three.

3. What if you disagree with the discussion?

Disagreements during a discussion are a natural part of the creative process. Whether you are problem-solving, discussing strategy or brainstorming, don't be afraid to challenge an idea. Even the most senior of executives don't know everything, and often you are closer to reality and have a valuable perspective to share.

Giving an alternative argument while still respecting the other person is a skill worth practising. Start by acknowledging the other person's idea and any part of it you agree is correct. Doing this ensures the other person feels listened to and respected. Then state your opinion using facts and logic rather than getting personal.

The use of 'I' statements such as or 'I believe', 'I suggest' or 'I'm concerned that' avoids people taking your point as a personal attack and getting defensive. You don't want to sound apologetic for having a different opinion, but being polite and not blaming the other person, means your point is likely to be heard.

Another essential aspect of disagreeing with someone is knowing when to back down. If you are passionate about your idea or opinion, it can feel uncomfortable to call it quits. However, there is no benefit from continuing to force your point. It is much more effective to take the debate offline or recognise that this is an argument you cannot win.

4. Dealing with interruptions

Research by Tonja Jacobi and Dylan Schweers at Northwestern University in Chicago[xxiii] studied the number and types of interruptions by Supreme Court judges.

Jacobi and Schweers reported that male justices interrupted female justices three times as much as the other way around, whatever the seniority. It may come as no surprise to you, but are you aware that not all interruptions are a bad thing?[xxiv]

Positive interruptions:

- Agreement – to back up or support your idea
- Assistance – to help by sharing a word or fact you were looking for, anyone with the menopause foggy memory will appreciate this one!
- Clarification – to gain a better understanding, which may help others too

Negative interruptions:

- Disagreement – jumping in to give a different opinion before you have finished
- Taking the floor - taking over the discussion but staying on the same subject
- Changing direction – introducing a new topic and dismissing your point
- Summarising – giving a summary of your position and perhaps minimising it

One of the reasons behind women experiencing a higher level of interruptions is that men tend to communicate for power, whereas women are more likely to talk for connection.

If you listen to a group of women talking, they generally use a soft language pattern, are inclusive, ask questions and allow brief gaps between speaking to enable others to respond without having to interrupt.

In contrast, a group of men talking will speak over each other, rarely ask questions, and there are no gaps between statements. This transactional style of communication isn't true of all men, and all women don't use the relational form either, but it's a general pattern and an interesting one to study.

What can you do if you're interrupted?

If you find you are regularly being interrupted, then there are several things you can do.

1. Determine if the interruption has a positive or negative intention. Is the person interrupting to support you, clarifying a point or are they cutting you off?
2. Then ask yourself, is this a battle I want to fight? Have you almost finished your point anyway or is the discussion too essential to get distracted?
3. Keep talking and increase your volume. You may feel that this sounds aggressive, but it may be important to finish your point, and most interrupters don't realise what they are doing.
4. Call it out. Phrases like, 'Can you wait a moment I haven't finished yet' or, 'I'm keen to hear your point, but I'm not done yet'.

How to avoid being interrupted

Rather than having to deal with interruptions, it can be easier to develop techniques to avoid being interrupted in the first place.

My clients find these techniques helpful:

1. Set an expectation of what you are going to say, such as, 'I have three comments on this, which will take a minute to share...' This statement prevents the interrupter from jumping in at the first break.
2. Be concise by keeping your points short and use smaller sentences. Then there is less opportunity for an interrupter to jump in.
3. Speak only when you have something of value to contribute. If you are waffling or have the reputation of talking for the sake of it, others will feel justified in interrupting you.
4. Take it offline, if someone is repeatedly interrupting you and others, talk to them privately. They may not be aware of their behaviour. Alternatively ask others for support, such as the facilitator of the meeting or other colleagues. They can 'amplify' your point by repeating your comment and crediting it to you before anyone else interrupts.

What if you want to interrupt?

There are some situations when no matter how uncomfortable interrupting feels; it is the right thing to do. To make sure you do it respectfully, consider these points:

1. Think twice, check in with yourself, do you have a critical point that you want to make at this moment, or could it wait?

2. Ask for permission, for example, 'Can I interrupt for a minute?' This question acknowledges the fact you are interrupting, showing respect to the person speaking and demonstrating that you are listening.

3. Increase your volume and use confident body language. If you are trying to make a point and the person speaking is not allowing you a way in, speaking louder than usual and leaning forward with an open body language indicates you are interrupting.

4. Acknowledge the speaker, by building on a point made by the person speaking; you can interrupt while being supportive You could use the phrase, 'That is a great point, X. I would like to add…'

Even when you dare to speak up and make your point, there is another unconscious bias preventing women from being heard positively. This was highlighted in research by Elizabeth McClean for the Academy of Management in 2017[xxv].

The study showed that when men suggest positive ideas or solutions, their leadership evaluation rises, but the same doesn't happen for women. This cultural stereotyping is an obstacle for women but can be overcome by:

- Women (and men) endorsing and advocating for each other
- Learning the art of speaking with authority and demonstrating expertise

- Increasing the number of women in leadership and expert positions

Client Story: Lesley

I was recommended to Lesley by one of my previous clients who I had helped become comfortable at contributing and challenging in meetings.

Lesley worked in the insurance business and had moved to a new company 6 months ago. She attended a lot of meetings about policy and procedures and client management, and although she had expertise in specific areas, she was junior in age and experience to a lot of the others participating.

Lesley told me she rarely spoke in these meetings except when she was directly asked a question on her specialist area. Even then, she felt uncomfortable as she lacked confidence in her knowledge and believed it was essential to know 100% of the information. Lesley had lost touch with her nugget of self-worth and as a result didn't see her value as equal to others in a meeting.

As you can probably recognise, Lesley was held back by 5 of the worries I previously mentioned, which were:

1. I don't want to say the wrong thing or appear stupid
2. I have nothing to add of value
3. I should be respectful to my seniors; their opinion is more important than mine
4. I don't have as much knowledge or experience as them; I should just listen
5. I should know the answers to all their questions as I'm the expert

We discussed the power Lesley had in those meetings, just by being invited to attend, that her specialist knowledge gave her the right to contribute, and her perception of the business meant she did have value to add.

As Lesley rarely spoke up, she didn't have the issues of being interrupted or dismissed. So, we started by agreeing on an intention for Lesley in those meetings.

Her first intentions may seem basic but when you lack confidence, taking some small steps rather than jumping straight in can be helpful. Lesley started by challenging herself to demonstrate confidence in her answers to questions. She did this by using confident body language, eye contact and a firm vocal tone (I cover this in Chapter 12 – Communicating with Power).

As well as this, Lesley found using the phrase, 'In my experience..' or, 'From working with…' enabled her to speak with authority. We then worked on her belief that as the expert, she must know everything. This belief put her under enormous pressure and meant she spent hours in preparation for any meeting. Lesley started to recognise that an 'expert' isn't expected to know everything and that it is okay to say you'll get back to them, rather than waffling an answer and feeling bad about yourself.

Once she was confident with answering questions, we moved on to how to contribute to the rest of the meeting, beginning with asking questions to clarify her understanding and progressing to giving her opinion by building on other people's points.

Lesley is not and does not want to be the loudest person at the table, but she now confidently takes her seat and speaks up when she has value to add. A role that has seen her be not only recognised for her contributions but rewarded too.

Self-Coaching Activity

1. In what type of meeting do you hold yourself back? Who is attending, what is the purpose, and what is your role?
2. Which of the common beliefs about speaking up worry you?
3. If you knew that all of these worries were false and that you had equal power to share your ideas, what would you do differently?
4. Think about what you bring to the meeting, is it knowledge, passion, a different perspective, a focus on detail or something else?
5. Set yourself an intention for the next meeting, for example – to give an opinion when you are not sure it is right, to challenge when you disagree with a point or to call out an interrupter.

In A Nutshell

- You have equal power to contribute to a meeting as anyone else invited. Don't give away that power to others because you are there to give your unique perspective.
- Many common beliefs hold women back from speaking up. You can overcome these by preparing well, setting an intention and having the courage to take a risk.

- Disagreements are part of a creative and problem-solving process. Don't take them personally and if you want to disagree use facts and logic.

- Interruptions will happen in some types of meetings (the rugby game). Choosing your battles is important, but so is calling out repeated interrupters.

Chapter 8

Coming Out of The Shadows

"I decided long ago never to walk in anyone's shadow. If I fail or if I succeed, at least I did as I believe."
Whitney Houston

I have mentioned many times in this book that in today's workplace culture, it isn't enough to work hard and deliver well. You also need to be visible, to demonstrate your confidence and potential and to be able to articulate your achievements and vision.

Being visible is easy to understand in principle, but what does it mean?

Ask yourself, do my peers, managers and senior execs know who I am, what my skills and expertise are and what I have achieved?

If the answer is no, then you have a real opportunity to raise your visibility.

You might be the hardest worker in your company, get on well with your colleagues and your boss may appreciate you at your performance review – but if you aren't at the front of senior people's minds, you will miss out on new opportunities, new projects, additional responsibilities and recognition.

They are all busy people under a lot of pressure to achieve their goals and objectives. That means they don't always have the time to be aware of the successes and effort put in by their team members. It is up to you to find ways of being noticed and standing out.

Career visibility is often talked about as a way to achieve career progression, but in a time when job security is not as strong as it has been, being visible in your organisation can support you in retaining your current role as well.

It doesn't stop there though. Getting noticed in your company is one thing, it is also helpful to be visible in your industry. By having a strong reputation or expertise externally, you will be aware of new opportunities, the strategic direction of the industry and the key movers and shakers. This is beneficial not only to you but also to your company and will raise your visibility both internally and externally.

How do you build your visibility?

There are so many different opportunities to raise your profile, and they vary according to your profession and company. I've shared a number of them here, but don't be scared to think 'out of the box' and create other scenarios that suit you and your organisation.

One of the biggest pushbacks I get from clients is, 'I'm overloaded with work already, I have no time for this!' I remind them that building your visibility should be seen as part of your job description. It is not something that you can do once you have cleared your desk of everything else. It needs to be prioritised and planned for, or you will not give it the importance it deserves.

A lack of time is a very common excuse or avoidance tactic for not doing something that takes you out of your comfort zone. Check-in with yourself, is that what you are doing?

Internal opportunities:

1. **Volunteer for more responsibility**

If you feel you have skills that are being underutilised or not being seen, then offering to take some workload off your manager or additional responsibilities to support the team gives you the perfect way to show them off.

Think about what precisely you could do and which of your skills this will showcase or develop, before approaching your boss or senior management.

A word of caution here - you shouldn't take on so much extra responsibility that your core job suffers. Also, avoid being pulled into obligations that are known as 'housekeeping' or go under most people's radar. These roles are anything from organising the Christmas party to attending conferences of little benefit to the company.

2. **Get involved in new projects**

New projects offer a fabulous opportunity for you to be innovative and creative. They also allow you to demonstrate leadership skills and project management.

Research how projects are assigned in your company or department, and make it known that you are interested when the next one comes up.

New projects can be risky as they don't always succeed, but that doesn't mean your visibility will be negative, as having the confidence to take a calculated risk is a leadership skill.

Ideally, the project you are part of would be high-profile across the business or have a significant impact on the bottom line.

Taking on a project that no one else wants to do is another way of getting recognised. The project goal could be tricky, or the subject matter unexciting, but by succeeding in a task or project like this, you will be highly valued, and if it doesn't work out, you have shown that you are willing to try to solve complicated issues.

3.   Represent your boss and department

In most companies, there are forums, meetings, conferences etc. that are cross-functional within the business.

Offering to represent your department or project in these situations is a fantastic way of getting seen by other parts of the organisation. You will be able to develop relationships and be exposed to new strategic information.

Once people in different departments know you, you are far more likely to be mentioned when an opportunity comes up.

Ensure you prepare well for the meetings and that you 'keep your power'. If speaking up is an issue for you, take a look back at the last chapter.

4.   Look out for opportunities to present

Is doing a presentation something you love or hate?

Being in front of an audience and sharing your expertise is an excellent way of becoming visible to several people in one go. Whether you are presenting to a small team or a full auditorium, look for potential situations to share your knowledge.

If you find doing a talk nerve wracking, then start small and build your confidence. Focus on what you want to share with the audience and the gift of knowledge you are giving them, rather than on your performance.

Having the opportunity to present to the board is very important. If you are involved in the work that is discussed with the exec, then ask to be part of the presentation. It will not only raise your visibility but also ensure you get credit for the work you've done.

5.   Find a mentor and sponsor

A mentor and sponsor are usually two separate people. A mentor is an experienced and trusted advisor who gives you support and helps build your skills. They are someone to turn to as a sounding board or for counsel when you have challenging issues and are generally empathetic.

A sponsor is someone senior to you who will advocate for your abilities and potential when you are not in the room. As Sylvia Hewlett, CEO of CTI – The Centre for Talent Innovation[xxvi], says, "Sponsors have three attributes. They believe in your potential and are prepared to take a bet on you; they have a voice at the table and are willing to be your champion; and they provide you with the cover you need, to take risks necessary to succeed. While mentors listen, sponsors act — by telling you what you need to know, clearing obstacles from your path, and making your success their business."

Do you have a mentor or sponsor to support you?

6.   Treat your area as your own business

Elena Bajic CEO of Ivy Exec[xxvii], says, "If your department or group within the company were your own business, how would you grow the bottom line - by increasing sales? Cutting costs? Ramping up efficiency?"

When you think of it as your own business, it gives you the motivation to spot problems others are ignoring and to be creative in suggesting solutions. For example, a client I worked with was frustrated that a change programme introduced by the company was not being implemented consistently by senior leaders. Rather than moaning to colleagues about it, she proactively went to her boss and suggested she do some research across the teams to understand the issues and come up with a solution.

As a result, she was able to interact with members of upper management she had not worked with before, and her visibility was sky high.

7.   Build a network internally

Putting the time into relationship building is an integral part of any job as it creates allies, enables you to accumulate knowledge, and allows you to help other areas which may then reciprocate your help.

You may feel that you have no specific purpose for meeting people in other divisions, but by being prepared with questions to help you understand their goals and issues, you will quickly fall into rapport with them.

8. Self-promotion

Self-promotion is a word that strikes fear into many career women. I cover this in detail in chapter ten and explain how it is possible to share your successes authentically and comfortably.

External Opportunities:

1. Become a networker

In some industries such as Law and Pharmaceuticals, there are lots of opportunities to network with others in the profession and potential new clients.

Knowing who the 'movers and shakers' in your industry are and the type of events that they attend is important. I cover this in detail in chapter fourteen.

2. Attend Events

As well as simple networking, does your industry have events such as conferences or professional development days? These enable you to network as well as learn about new developments.

Even better is to volunteer to present at one of these events to establish your position as an expert in that area and get high visibility for you and your company.

3. Get quoted or published

Does your industry have a professional or trade magazine/s, online or in print?

Research the types of articles that are published and make contact with the editor to suggest one you have written.

Alternatively, has something newsworthy happened in your company? Can you get it into a publication, with a quote from you?

4. Serve on an association or committee

Being involved in your professional industry association or sitting on a committee making decisions about the profession is a fantastic way to get your name noticed. It requires a commitment of time and effort, but the visibility will be a career accelerator.

5. Use social media

Your company may have a marketing department and a social media feed of their own, but platforms like LinkedIn and Twitter are both tools you can personally use for professional visibility.

I don't want you to feel overwhelmed by all these ideas. Taking action on any of them is a step forward. Prioritise the ones you think will have the most significant impact, but check in with yourself that you are still going out of your comfort zone.

Client Story: Sunita

Sunita worked in the pharmaceutical industry and had made steady career progress to a senior level. Her next step was to become a Director and to reach this, she will need to step up her visibility and demonstrate her potential.

Our specific goal working together was to achieve visibility with the senior exec and to feel comfortable giving her input at that level.

My first step was to uncover the beliefs that Sunita had around being visible that were holding her back. As with many of my clients, it stemmed from childhood conditioning about being modest and respecting elders and betters. She also didn't understand why what she delivered was not enough to get her recognised and visible. She felt strongly that it shouldn't be the case, and it jarred with her values of fairness and justice.

In our discussions, Sunita was able to identify situations where less competent colleagues had been promoted above her. She then had the insight that it was their ability to network, self-promote and be visible to the right people that had made the difference.

As I explained that being visible doesn't mean you have to 'play a part' or be pushy, she realised that visibility could be achieved authentically.

Sunita felt most comfortable bringing visibility to herself via her team and her work. We created ways in which she could use the team's profile to boost her own, for example, volunteering the team for a specific project that was highly visible.

I encouraged her to proactively seek out openings to present her work to the senior exec and follow this up with individual meetings to get feedback.

As Sunita's confidence grew, so did the opportunities to be visible and I am pleased to say that Sunita has reached that director position, deservedly so in my opinion.

Self-Coaching Activity

1. Read through the visibility opportunities I have listed above and add to them any other possible situations that you could use to increase your visibility.
2. Using a traffic light system, score yourself on how much you are making of each opportunity. A red light means not at all, an amber light means I do it sometimes but could improve, a green light means you are making great use of this idea already and need to continue.
3. Look at the red lights first and ask yourself, 'What is it that holds me back from doing this?' Is it the excuse of lack of time, do you think the impact on your career will be minimal, or is it the uncomfortable belief that you will come across as pushy? When you have an honest answer, either plan some small steps you can make towards it or move on to the next red light. Follow this by looking at any amber lights and decide if putting more effort into these options will increase your visibility.

4. Hopefully, you will now have a plan of action for visibility. I suggest you find some support to ensure you achieve your goals. Your mentor, sponsor, boss or an accountability buddy are ideal for this.

In A Nutshell

- It's not enough to work hard and deliver well, to achieve career progression you also need to be visible.
- There are lots of options both internally and externally to help you in getting noticed for the right reasons, which ones will you use?
- See getting visible as part of your job description, not something you will do when you have time.
- Opportunities will not usually be handed to you to increase your visibility. You need to be proactive and make them yourself.

Chapter 9

Develop Your Personal Brand

"To be nobody but yourself in a world which is doing its best, night and day, to make you everybody else, means to fight the hardest battle which any human being can fight; and never stop fighting."
E. E. Cummings

> *A personal brand can sound like another corporate buzz word or feel like another 'should' to add to your already overwhelming to-do list, but when you understand what a personal brand is and how you uncover it, you will realise how thought-provoking and beneficial it can be.*

As Maggie Eyre says in her book *Being You*[xxviii], "A personal brand tells the world about who you are as a human being personally and professionally."

She also says, "Sadly, the term personal brand is also confused with blatant self-promotion or a cynical way to market oneself as someone you are not."

That may be true for some people, but your personal brand can be unique, authentic and honest. It will come from a combination of your values, strengths, purpose, legacy and personality, and be genuinely you.

111

Why bother with a personal brand?

There are many reasons for having a personal brand, and to me, the most important ones are:

1. To make your CV and interview style stand out from others, giving you the best chance of landing that new job or promotion.
2. To have an online presence that reflects your personal brand. According to CareerBuilder, "More than half of employers won't hire potential candidates without some online presence today".
3. To help you market yourself in your current and future companies to achieve the career progression you are looking for.
4. To stop other people defining your personal brand for you. If you are unsure what is unique about you and what you would like others to think of you, then they will make their assumptions, and it may not be a description you want.
5. Would you like to be involved in your external industry? It could be in presentations, committees or associations. Having a personal brand that others recognise is essential for this.
6. If you are looking to freelance, have your own company or be a CEO someday, then you will accelerate your path with a great personal brand. Brandyourself.com describes a recent study from Weber Shandwick[xxix], in which global executives attribute 45% of their company's reputation to the reputation of their CEO.

Getting started on your personal brand

When I work with clients on their personal brand, I like to start with clarifying their core values. Your core values are the beliefs and principles that make you uniquely who you are.

Some values are embedded in us during our upbringing and create the way we perceive the world and react to situations. Other values come about through our exposure to life's experiences and can change as we move into different phases of our life.

When your core values are met, you feel in balance and fulfilled. If they are out of balance, you may be uncomfortable and tend towards frustration and anxiety.

By identifying your core values, you can understand your behaviour and reactions and more easily connect with your golden nugget of self-worth. You then have the choice to adapt your life to feel in balance with them.

For example, I have a strong value of respect, and for some reason, I link respect to punctuality. When I meet friends, and they arrive late, I feel disproportionately upset about it. I now recognise that I'm feeling disrespected and that the situation has triggered my respect value.

Knowing this doesn't change the situation or feeling, but does allow me to see their perspective. Respect may not be a core value of theirs so they probably don't link it to punctuality, so I let it go.

Discover Your Core Values

Step 1 – Empty your mind

If you feel you know what your core values are already, this is the time to get them down on paper and empty your mind. It is worth then carrying on to the other steps to see if they remain the same.

If you have no idea of your core values that's fine - just move onto Step 2.

Step 2 – Choose your values

Look through the list of suggested values below and circle those that are important to you.

Remember there are no 'shoulds' in this exercise. You may see values you think you 'should' have but make sure you only circle those that you believe are important to you.

The definition and meaning you put on each word are personal to you, and again, there is no right or wrong.

Add any from step 1 that aren't listed or any others you want to include.

Loyalty	Innovation	Integrity	Security
Fun	Honesty	Respect	Adventure
Resourcefulness	Acceptance	Creativity	Peace
Altruism	Contentment	Commitment	Fairness
Cooperation	Dependability	Service	Support
Caring	Strength	Courage	Accountability
Loyalty	Persistence	Faith	Order
Humour	Trust	Justice	Authenticity
Dignity	Honour	Flexibility	Learning
Spirituality	Collaboration	Excellence	Freedom
Quality	Achievement	Balance	Empathy

Positivity	Generosity	Vitality	Open-mindedness
Risk	Sensuality	Humility	Expertise
Wisdom	Teaching	Organisation	Understanding
Curiosity	Independence	Power	Beauty
Gratitude	Stability	Vision	Contentment
Coach	Inspiration	Connection	Joy
Inspiration	Self-worth	Presence	Strength
Truth	Innovation	Integrity	Security

Step 3 – Overlaps

You may have noticed that some of the values overlap with others. Have a look at your list of circled values and determine if any of them are similar, e.g. justice and fairness. Then cross out the value that means the least to you.

Step 4 – Determining your top values

Review your remaining values and choose your top 6 to 8.
Asking yourself the following questions can help:

- Which values are essential to my life?
- Which values represent how I am in the world?
- Which values do I need to feel fulfilled?

Step 5 – Ordering

Arrange your core values with the most important at the top
and then complete the table below. Enter your interpretation
of the value and how well it is being met from 1 to 10 (1 =
not at all; 10 = totally met). Consider both how well you are
meeting it and how well others meet it in your score.

Value	My Interpretation	Level my value is met
Respect	*Showing respect to others and also my thoughts and feelings*	7

You have now clarified your values and thought about which ones are in balance in your life and which ones need work. Does this explain why you feel uncomfortable at times? Reflect on these scores and ask yourself what you can do to move each value's score up just one number.

The next step is moving on to look at your strengths.

Your personal and professional strengths

For this exercise, I would like you to pick five significant people in your professional and personal life, at least three of whom know you in a work capacity.

Ask each of them to tell you what they believe are your three greatest strengths. People generally respond quite happily to this request as you are focusing on the positives.

Try to choose individuals who you feel most uncomfortable asking, rather than going for your closest friends and family.

While you are waiting for them to come back to you, reflect on what you believe are your personal and professional strengths. Have these changed over time? Which are you most proud of? Do any of them set you apart from your colleagues and peers?

When you have received your feedback – did any of it surprise you? You will probably find some themes coming out, which will help further develop your personal brand.

Individual	Strength

What is your life purpose?

The idea of having a purpose in life might sound grandiose and self-indulgent to some, but for others, it gives them a real focus on their career and personal life.

Our ability as humans to self-reflect means that we can ponder such things as our purpose. It is innate in our make-up, so why not give it a go?

Your life purpose is about who you are and not what you do. It is your reason for being and the impact you have on the world in which you live. Being clear on your life purpose can be a powerful guide and driver in your career and life.

It doesn't have to be something with a profound impact like 'world peace', it can also be something personal to you or the ones you love.

To help you draw out your life purpose, I'm going to share with you a three visualisations. This exercise comes from Firework Career Coaching Programme[xxx], of which I am a certified coach.

Revealing your life purpose

Find yourself somewhere comfortable to sit with a pen and paper and get yourself relaxed. Read through the first visualisation, then close your eyes and imagine yourself in that situation.

1. 95th Birthday Party

It is your 95th birthday party; you are happy, healthy and robust. There is a party in your garden, and all your friends, family and people you have enjoyed working with have come. As you sit watching them, people come up to you and thank you for what you have meant to them in their life. Sit and listen to the words they say.

Once you have completed the visualisation, immediately write down the words and descriptions you heard.

Then move on to number two.

2. Peak Experience

Think of a peak experience you had in your life, something that meant a lot to you. Look back at the experience and notice how you feel and what you see. What was your unique role in the situation? How were you acting? What kind of impact were you having on others?

Again, as soon as you have finished the visualisation, write down what you heard, saw and felt.

Now move on to visualisation three.

3. 15-Minute TV Slot

You've been given a 15-minute slot on TV at peak time. It's your chance to communicate with millions of people and it's guaranteed to have a big impact. You can use it anyway you feel like. What would you use it to say? What words and images would you use? What would your closing message be?

Make a note of the words and images you come up with.

Now look back at your notes. What themes can you notice? What is the impact you are having on the world, people or yourself?

Reflect on what you have discovered and have a go at forming a purpose statement - a simple phrase that feels meaningful to you. Don't worry if nothing comes immediately, give your thoughts time to settle down and you will probably find an idea will pop up when you were not expecting it.

You'll know when you have found the right words for you because you'll fall into the same feeling as when you connect with your self-worth.

Here are some of my client's purpose statements:

My life purpose is to wake people up to their potential

I am the rock for my family

I want to inspire others that however difficult their life is they can still achieve great things

I want to be a role model in my career

My purpose is to make a difference to others however big or small

What is your Career Legacy?

According to Next Avenue contributor Phyllis Weiss Haserot in *Forbes*[xxxi], "Almost everyone wants to leave some sort of legacy at work – to be remembered for something meaningful."

For those coming towards retirement or about to transition career, the wish to leave a career legacy is stronger. It is also an essential thing to consider in defining your personal brand.

The difficulty comes in how to identify your legacy and then how to deliver it. As Phyllis says, "Work legacy can be about such things as creating new work processes, mentoring and transferring knowledge to younger employees and training new talent. It's what you pass on to the next generations and your peers in as broad a sense as you would like."

To be able to work out your personal brand, it isn't essential to have nailed down your legacy. Having an idea of what you would like to be remembered for by your colleagues, clients, stakeholders and industry experts is very helpful, though.

Consider these questions to help you:

- What would have been helpful for you when you first started your career?

- What, if anything, has held you back in achieving the career success you would like to achieve?
- What projects or changes did you feel were important but never completed for reasons out of your control?
- What is it about your role models or people in the industry that you respect? Could that be your legacy too?

What is your personality?

Lastly, I would like you to consider your personality traits. Which ones are essential to include in your personal brand, if you haven't already?

You may want to include themes such as the Big 5 personality traits[xxxii].
These are the 5 categories of personality traits which were developed by the research of D. W. Fiske (1949) and later expanded upon by other researchers including Norman (1967), Smith (1967), Goldberg (1981), and McCrae & Costa (1987).

- Openness
- Conscientiousness
- Extraversion
- Agreeableness
- Neuroticism

If you have reached this point in the chapter, then well done! These exercises require a lot of self-reflection and navel-gazing.

You are finally at the point where you can articulate your personal brand.

How you describe your personal brand is your choice and will vary by situation. I suggest you look over all the words and ideas you have written down. Which of them make you feel proud? Which would you pick as your USP – Unique Selling Point - compared to your peers?

Some of my clients like to have just a few words that sum up their personal brand, for example: strategic, relationship-building and collaborative, or: inspiring, innovative, decisive and authentic.

If you want to incorporate your personal brand into your CV or resume, you need to make it a longer statement that tells a story and sells you.

Here is an example of a personal statement on a CV[xxxiii]:

Target-oriented Sales Executive with a 15-year sales record. Proven success in both B2B and B2C verticals. Grew [Company X] client base from 10 to 50 within one year. Increased sales by 40 per cent by implementing a new lead qualification tool. As a confident networker, brings to the table effective relationships with key senior contacts in FTSE 250 organisations.

With your LinkedIn Profile, your personal brand should come out in your headline and summary. The summary gives you 2000 characters to sell yourself, although many people recruiters say they only look at the first 300.

Below is my LinkedIn summary as an example. Bear in mind, it is written to attract clients rather than recruiters. I intended to get across elements of my personal brand. They include my passion for helping women, my experience with thousands of clients, my media presence and the key areas I support women in – being heard, overcoming self-doubts and marketing themselves.

As the UK's leading Career, Leadership and Confidence Coach, I'm passionate about working with senior women who are looking to progress their career and are frustrated at being held back by their mindset or the culture at work.

I've worked with thousands of professional women often in male-dominated industries who feel they're not getting the progress, recognition and fulfilment they deserve.

You can watch my masterclass on The 4 Steps To Get More Recognition and Impacyt At Work Without Being Seen As Bossy or Pushy' on my YouTube channel Jo Painter

In my 17 years working in a FTSE 100 company, I witnessed many women being held back by their inner critical voice, their need to fit in and be liked, and by the workplace culture. These feelings meant they struggled in situations where they felt intimidated, inexpert or lacked self-belief.

As a result, I'm passionate about supporting senior women through executive coaching or career coaching to feel recognised, valued and fulfilled at work. I've spent years researching and developing my programmes, and the results they've achieved are amazing!

My clients have gone from feeling stuck, frustrated and undervalued to getting promotions, pay rises and fulfilling their potential WITHOUT spending years getting burnt out or sacrificing who they are.

Clients who work with me typically:

- Get their voice heard and get credit for their ideas and achievements

- Stop self-sabotaging and gain unshakeable confidence

- Feel comfortable marketing and promoting themselves

I appear regularly in the press, on Sky News and various PR campaigns. I've worked with many organisations such as Amazon, Ford and Lloyds Banking Group speaking about the challenges for women in the workplace and how they can overcome them.

I'd love to help you achieve the results my clients got, and you can arrange a chat with me by messaging me on LinkedIn or booking a free call on my online calendar at www.speakwithjo.com

With social media, it is also worthwhile going back over your previous posts and comments to ensure there is nothing that directly goes against the personal brand you want to portray.

Client Story: Amanda

Amanda had a very senior role in a large American corporation, which she had achieved through her personal drive, problem-solving abilities and emotional intelligence.

She was now aiming at her first executive board role and came to work with me on her visibility, self-belief and executive presence – the X-factor that inspires loyalty and delivery.

Working on her personal brand was one aspect of her programme and the self-reflection Amanda underwent gave her some of the most significant insights and mindset changes she achieved.

As with many clients I talk to, Amanda felt that to reach the executive level, she would have to demonstrate the leadership behaviours of the majority of the exec. This idea did not sit well for Amanda, and she was struggling to see how her authentic style could fit in.

As Amanda gained clarity on her personal brand, she began to value the parts of her brand that were unique to her. She could see how her behaviours of challenging the status quo and innovation would drive the business forward, but also how her empathy and influencing of leaders would set her apart from her peers.

This month Amanda has just started her new role on the executive board and who knows where the rest of her career will take her.

Self-Coaching Activity

There are already a large number of exercises in this chapter for you to complete. Therefore my only suggestions for you to build on these are:

1. When you have defined your personal brand, test it out with friends and colleagues you trust. Do they feel it describes and 'sells' you?
2. Your personal brand may develop as your career does. Ensure you regularly refresh it, to keep it authentic and real.

In A Nutshell

*   A personal brand tells the world who you are personally and professionally.
*   The purpose of the personal brand is to market you consistently and authentically and lead to career success, whatever that means to you.
*   You can define your personal brand using your values, strengths, purpose, legacy and personality.
*   Once you have your personal brand, you can use it in networking, on social media, in job applications and everyday work.

Chapter 10

The Art of Self-Promotion (without being a bragger)

I have a teenage daughter and son, and I believe we have encouraged them equally to have confidence and self-belief throughout their upbringing. What is interesting is the different behaviours that they demonstrate around their abilities and achievements.

My son will come home from an exam saying how well it went and that he thinks he's done really well and to be honest he probably has. Whereas my daughter will come back from an exam unsure and down on herself, saying some of it was really tough and she doesn't think she's got a high score.

Academically they are very similar and are likely to get around the same results. My daughter will be pleased with herself and excitedly tell me about it but won't mention it to anyone else unless asked. She may also then start to worry about what she needs to do to get such a good result next time.

My son will have compared his results with his friends and if he has scored higher, he will be what we describe as 'full of himself'. He'll announce his results to us with a 'what else did you expect?' tone and be very comfortable to talk about them to anyone.

Does that resonate with you or your children? I was shocked to see the gender differences at such an early stage. Why do we as women find it particularly hard to advocate for ourselves and talk about our achievements?

I believe this comes back to what we discussed in Chapter Two about 'nice girl' conditioning and Chapter Eight on visibility. In the chapters I explained the issue of women believing that their work will speak for itself and that there is no need to self-promote. I also shared how our early years conditioning to be nice, modest and not blow your own trumpet adds to this lower confidence level.

There are four other reasons I have found that commonly hold my clients back from self-promoting. These are:

1. A fear of being seen as a bragger

Can you recall a situation where you experienced a senior colleague bragging or boasting about their achievements and abilities? Or have you moaned with friends about a colleague that always tries to take credit for your work and talks themselves up?

Those sorts of cringeworthy experiences can reinforce the belief that you must not brag or talk about 'I' instead of 'we', or others will see you as arrogant and boastful.

The problem with this is that it isn't an all or nothing situation. It's not a case of either I say nothing at all or I am a bragger. Instead there is a big grey area in between the black and white of bragger and silent. If you were to start sharing your successes a little and taking credit for the work you have done, you would still be nowhere near the bragging level you are scared of.

Don't let the fallacy that all promotional behaviour is bad stop you using this effective tool for career progression.

2. Lack of a role model

In my experience there are relatively few successful women out there that demonstrate the skill of effective self-promotion. Part of the reason for this was highlighted in a study as far back as 1997.

Laurie Redman of New Jersey University found that self-promotion for women was a double-edged sword[xxxiv]. When women shared their successes it substantially improved the perception of their competence, however it also reduced their social acceptance or likeability.

As Laurie says in her conclusion, this means that when women don't self-promote they risk damaging their professional success as they are not challenging the gender stereotype. If they do self-promote they risk jeopardising their social success for not fitting the likeability expectation of the gender stereotype.

This is an unfair no-win situation for women. The solution many women find is to walk a tightrope between sharing their success, while being caring and kind.

You can probably understand now why there aren't many female role models who have successfully balanced this double bind. Without examples to copy and learn from it is not surprising that the majority of us haven't become comfortable with dropping our modesty.

3. Self-Sabotaging

Self-sabotaging behaviour is one that causes you some form of pain and stops you achieving the things you want to. In this particular example I am referring to the self-sabotaging thinking that stops you from sharing your successes.

The classic types of self-sabotaging behaviour at work here are: worrying what others think, overthinking and ruminating, and a fear of being judged.

It might be helpful here to share with you the difference between self-promotion and bragging:

- **Self-promotion** is talking about your performance with facts and being able to back up what you are saying
- **Bragging** is about exaggerating and making yourself sound better than you are. It's claiming you have achievements or abilities without any evidence to prove it. People who feel the need to brag often have insecurities they are trying to keep hidden.

For example, to say you and your team have achieved the top sales for the month would be a fact and therefore self-promotion. To say that the sales were all down to your expertise and you expected to be top every month, would be an exaggeration and bragging.

When you know you are sharing facts with evidence, you can be confident that you are not being boastful and that any negative reaction is down to the insecurities of others and out of your control.

4. Belief it's a masculine behaviour

Many women I have spoken to find the whole self-promotion piece to be a domain for males or traditional office politics that they don't want to be involved in. Tara Mohr refers to this in her book Playing Big[xxxv].

This belief is usually a result of seeing male colleagues bragging and trying to out-do each other. I can understand this feeling of not wanting to copy others' behaviour or to 'play the game', however as you will see below there are plenty of ways you can share your successes and still remain authentic to your own style.

How can I self-promote authentically?

As well as raising your profile and people's perception of your competence, self-promotion also gives you access to people and information that can impact your career. It gets you the visibility, which enables you to build relationships, learn about new areas and find new opportunities.

Even though you are promoting yourself authentically, it may still feel uncomfortable at first. Starting a new behaviour will always take some getting used to. I suggest you choose the approach from the following list that feels the most comfortable and make that your first challenge.

As you can see there are many different ways to self-promote; which of these resonates with you?

1. Know and promote your best skills and competences

This is your USP or personal brand. As we discussed in the last chapter your personal brand should be part of all your communication and interactions.

If your brand is around innovation and creativity and that is the direction you were looking to progress your career in, then your focus would be to gain visibility for your successful ideas. You could also look for opportunities to improve your understanding of the role and strategy in different areas of the business, to inform your innovations.

For a brand centred around collaboration and developing others, again you could highlight these particular aspects of your journey and successes. Volunteering for projects or to advise teams where these skills are essential gives you the chance to spotlight your skills.

2. Find opportunities in meetings

It might not feel appropriate to throw out an example of your achievements without context in a meeting but do look out for opportunities to share your successes as examples for problem solving and as learning points. You can also use questions as a way in, for example, 'Have you considered using X as a process? I found it very successful in a similar situation…' Having examples prepared beforehand can help give you the confidence to speak up.

3. Drop in on your boss to give an update

We assume that our managers know exactly what we are doing, the problems we have resolved and the achievements we have made. If you are a leader yourself you will know that a lot of your time and brain space is taken up with your own work and priorities. Regularly updating your boss with the journey and not just the results may seem unnecessary, but it does make a difference.

One of my clients hadn't realised how important it was until she was promoted. The colleague who stepped into her old role was seen as being amazing because she was constantly telling her manager about the great things she was doing, which impressed him. My client said none of this was new - she had been doing it for years but never talked about it!

We probably all know someone who is good at this, regularly telling their seniors about the small successes or progress markers they have delivered. Take the time to observe what they are doing and then find a balance that feels comfortable for you. Don't be put off by the worry that you are 'bothering' your boss; getting visible is an important part of your job.

4. Focus on the work

If all of this self-promotion feels very uncomfortable to you, then, to start with, think of it as promoting the impact of your work both current and future. The business could be missing out on your great ideas if you don't have the courage to make them visible.

Once you are comfortable with highlighting your work, you can start to bring the focus onto yourself as well.

5. Talk about the team and 'I'

You have probably heard the phrase there is no 'I' in team, but that doesn't mean you shouldn't talk about your specific role in the project as well as the team's achievement.

Imagine you've worked really hard with your colleague on a project to implement some new IT software in the company. It's achieved great success and you are asked to present how it went to the directors. You know your colleague is very good at talking herself up, how are you going to make sure you get equal credit?

This is an example of an opportunity to talk about your individual contribution as well as that of your team. By preparing this upfront you can ensure that you make the most of every opening.

Consider this example of how you could respond to the imaginary opportunity:

I'm really pleased with how the project went and we successfully achieved the KPIs we were aiming for. I focused on managing the behavioural change, which had a number of issues ... however, giving support and ensuring good communication has resulted in everyone being on board.

In this statement you've acknowledged the 'we' but also brought in your specific role with an 'I'. You have talked about the difficulties – i.e. the 'journey' and taken ownership for a specific part of the result. By describing the transferable skills you have used, it will also demonstrate your potential for the future.

6. Share collaboratively with peers

One of the issues I have found that stop people from sharing their successes is that they feel what they have achieved is not important enough or they achieved it too easily. It is important to remember that what felt simple to you may not to others who have a different set of skills.

That means if you share an achievement with your peers and seniors it can be done from a collaborative perspective rather than for the sake of bragging, in order to pass on your learning that will be useful for them too.

7.   Advocate for others

Advocating for someone means publicly supporting them. You can do this proactively by agreeing with other colleagues and speaking up for one another's successes, or on a more ad hoc basis when you feel a person or a success needs to be acknowledged.

Most women find it very easy to promote other people in comparison to doing it for themselves.

The power of this is that it avoids the backlash for women's likeability factor that can come from self-promotion. Also, if you advocate for someone they are far more likely to speak up for you in return.

8.   Ask for feedback on a good result

If your boss or senior knows about the result of a successful client interaction, but doesn't appear to value the result as much as you hoped, it may be that they are just not giving it their full attention.

You can bring focus to this success by asking your manager and key stakeholders for feedback on the process and your specific performance. This brings the success to the forefront of their mind, without you promoting it. It also allows you the chance to expand on details and the skills you have used to demonstrate your potential.

9. Take on new opportunities

By proactively taking on new opportunities you raise your profile and showcase your skills.

A good example of this was my client Josie, whose company asked for senior managers willing to be mentors. Josie was interested, however her boss said it was not really something they 'did' in sales and it probably wasn't worth applying. Josie applied anyway and became the first ever sales mentor. A fantastic way to demonstrate confidence, capability and courage.

10. Build relationships with other parts of the business

It may seem to you that there is little benefit in developing links with a totally separate division of the company. However, raising your profile in all areas of the organisation can not only open up new opportunities, it can also give you a broader knowledge of the business than your peers.

A useful way into this conversation can be to ask about their particular department's goals and issues and ask how you or your area could support them.

11. Don't miss 'How are you?' opportunities

Often the simplest approaches to self-promotion are the best. You may not always have the chance to speak to the exec by yourself or to have a one to one chat with visiting clients and colleagues. The 'how are you?' question can be a great way in.

Most of us would respond to the question with something like 'fine thanks, how are you?'. Polite, but not exactly a conversation to be remembered. Instead you could talk about the project you are currently working on, the issues you are having and the how you plan to overcome them.

For example, 'I'm doing well thanks, and I'm currently working on X. It has been difficult for the team due to Y, but we plan to overcome it with Z.'

My client, May, told me she found the most useful self-promotion strategy for her was when she went to the coffee machine and was asked casually by her colleagues or seniors as they were taking their coffee break, 'How are you doing?' This then gave her the opportunity to discuss something she was working on or had recently completed. Is this something you would feel comfortable doing?

12. Use internal communications

Most organisations have some form of communication that goes out to all employees. It could be an online update newsletter or an intranet service.

Making use of this allows you to self-promote without any of the discomfort of a face-to-face interaction. As I mentioned previously you can also promote your team here and include specifics about your role.

Ensure your article or update stands out from others by using photos or video and attention-grabbing headlines.

I know you are probably now thinking, 'Videos, updates in writing, scary!!!' and I've been there too. The first time I started putting videos on social media talking about my work and the clients I have helped, I was so uncomfortable. It took me weeks before I could listen to my voice or watch myself, but now it feels natural.

Don't let self-consciousness hold you back.

13. Networking

I have put all the focus so far on promoting yourself internally, but if you are looking to progress your career in your particular industry you will need to raise your profile externally too.

There are a number of ways to do this and I discuss networking in more detail in Chapter Twelve. Look out for opportunities to network such as:

- Industry conferences
- Industry networking events
- Professional association meetings and events
- Women only networks across various industries
- Talks
- Fundraising events
- Meetups
- Virtual online networking
- Volunteer opportunities

14. Become an expert

If you want to stand out externally it is helpful to become a specialist in a particular area within your industry. That doesn't mean you need to only talk about your particular niche, but by being recognised as having knowledge in that area you are automatically visible.

To be seen as a specialist involves sharing information about your area of knowledge. You can achieve this through writing professional articles, sitting on relevant, committees and speaking about your subject at conferences etc.

15. Social Media

Social media is generally something you love or hate. I have taught myself how to use social media to share my knowledge and connect with other women. However, I can appreciate that for some people it feels scary or dangerous, with the fear that you might say the wrong thing or be judged.

Most large organisations have their own marketing department and social media strategy [xxxvi]representing the company. You can still share your own information as long as you remember that your message will reflect on your company's image too.

I recommend to clients that they build a social media community, particularly on LinkedIn and Twitter, beginning by identifying the 'movers and shakers' in their industry and the people connected to them. Connecting with peers and other like-minded professionals can also provide a supportive community for you.

Commenting on and sharing content and opinions within your community will start to get your profile noticed. Then you can join and become active in relevant groups or begin a group of your own on LinkedIn if a suitable one doesn't exist. Finally, publishing your own articles will raise your profile and build your expertise.

As I mentioned in the chapter on visibility, most employers will now look at your online profile as part of the recruitment process. Making sure your online image meets your personal brand and appears professional is more important than ever.

16. Get distracted

A study by Jessi Smith and Megan Huntoon in 2013 [xxxvii] into 'Women's Bragging Rights' showed, unsurprisingly, that when women self-promote they feel internal stress and distraction.

As part of the study, they put a generator in the room which was making a lot of noise. The increase in ability to promote themselves with less stress was significant.

This study backs up the fact that when we are distracted, we come out of our own heads and come back to the present which means we worry less about sharing successes.

Client Story: Asha

Self-promotion is something that comes up for lots of my clients, but Asha stands out for me, as she was told to get some coaching specifically to develop this skill.

Her company paid for her coaching as they valued her, and recognised that not being visible would hold her back in her career.

Asha is an introvert and an intelligent and respected employee. She has been told that to progress she will need to raise her profile amongst the numerous directors and to instil the confidence in them that she can not only deliver in her current role but has the potential to take on a more strategic position.

We began by exploring Asha's discomfort around taking the credit for her work and marketing herself. Asha's cultural background had resulted in her carrying the belief that her opinions, work and self were less valuable than others. Despite logically knowing that her company's culture wasn't apparently biased in this way, she struggled to get past her own behaviours.

I discussed with Asha how this story she was holding onto about women and especially herself having less importance was fallacious. If she could recognise that only her thinking was keeping it in place, then she could be open to showing her abilities to the world.

It took a few sessions, but once Asha saw it for herself, it was as if a door had opened and she could step out and be herself.

I would love to say she then straightaway felt the freedom to be visible and promote herself. However, years of being modest and humble meant that she had to build her confidence one step at a time.

We developed a plan to enable her to authentically become visible and self-promote. She began by sharing her team's achievements, sharing new ideas, or speaking up when she disagreed with another opinion,. As her confidence built she volunteered to represent the department and present to the directors.

Asha consistently used social media to raise her profile externally and regularly attended industry events, rather than just going when she had to. By overcoming her discomfort around seniority, she relaxed enough to be able to chat about her successes and issues.

Finally, she had the best piece of feedback: she was asked to apply for a senior role and got it.

Self-Coaching Activity

1. Have you clarified your personal brand? This is a core part of self-promotion so if not, take a look at Chapter Eight again
2. Build an 'achievement portfolio'. This sounds like a lot of work but is simply a mental or physical list of your accomplishments and capabilities. It is so easy

to just move on to the next problem after a success so taking the time to record your successes is essential. You will then have a regular reminder and not struggle to think of things to promote.

3. Ask yourself the following questions:
    I. What fear is holding you back from sharing your successes? Is it logical or emotional?
    II. Do you believe you are respected at work?
    III. If you respected a colleague or team member would you be interested to hear what they have achieved and what they learnt from it?
    IV. If you knew you would not be thought of as boastful or uninteresting, how would you promote myself?

4. Complete the self-promotion action plan over the page with 5 different activities you have committed to complete from the strategies above. Make comments about the situations you completed them in and how it went.

Self-Promotion Action Plan

Situation	Action	By When	Comments

In A Nutshell

- Self-promotion is habitually avoided and underestimated by career women, often due to experiencing other people bragging and boasting.
- Other reasons we don't share our successes are the lack of role models, 'nice' girl conditioning, believing our work should speak for itself and a self-sabotaging mindset.
- It is possible to self-promote authentically and without bragging.
- Identify the self-promotion strategy that feels most comfortable (or least uncomfortable) and have the courage to try it out. Remember that whatever you do at your core you are always okay.

Chapter 11

I'm Okay, You're Okay: How to be Assertive

"To be passive is to let others decide for you. To be aggressive is to decide for others. To be assertive is to decide for yourself. And to trust that there is enough, that you are enough."
Edith Eva Eger

Assertiveness

Assertiveness is a communication style that respects your opinions, thoughts and needs as well as those of others. Some people pick up the skill naturally, and others need to learn it.

As I mentioned previously, I had a very traditional upbringing, and while my mum was a wonderful, funny and kind woman, she was not assertive. She was a real people pleaser, putting everyone else's needs and wants before herself. This was a result of her upbringing, and probably her parents' before that. I, therefore, grew up without an example of an assertive woman. As a result, I had to learn how to be assertive. The good news is it's a skill you can definitely learn.

To describe assertiveness, I'll put it into context with what is generally recognised as the other three communication styles: passive, aggressive and passive aggressive[xxxviii].

For each behaviour I suggest you reflect on whether this is a style of communication you use and when you use it. There are situations where assertiveness is not the most appropriate behaviour.

Passive Communication

When you are passively communicating, it means you are not speaking up for your opinions, thoughts and needs. You don't react to hurtful or diminishing situations and instead swallow down your feelings. As a result, your resentments and anger build up inside, and at some point, in reaction to a minor trigger, you may explode with all the internalised feelings.

Because you are not vocalising your feelings, you may:

- Feel anxious and not in control
- Feel stuck and depressed
- Feel resentful that others get what they want
- Feel confused about how you do feel

Passive communication is known as the 'You Are Okay, I'm Not Okay' style. The other person is happy to be respected, but you feel undervalued.

In the longer term, the other person may be frustrated that all the decisions and opinions are theirs. That can cause your relationship to suffer.

If you are a passive communicator, you are likely to lack confidence, and your body language will demonstrate this.

Aggressive Communication

Aggressive communication, as you might expect, is the opposite of passive and is the 'I'm Okay, You Are Not Okay' style. You feel good as you have expressed your anger, but the other person is not okay. Your wants and needs have been met, but not theirs. After the interaction, you may feel guilty, and that leads to nobody being okay.

Have you ever been at the receiving end of aggressive behaviour? Whether it is an angry boss or a frustrated client, most of us have been verbally abused or bullied at some time. How did it make you feel? Did it have a long-term effect?

I remember, early on in my career, my boss once exploded over a calculation mistake I had made in a budget document that had already gone out to key stakeholders. His reaction, from my perspective, was utterly over the top and disproportionate to the impact of my mistake. I can still remember the stomach-churning emotional response I had to his aggression. Being a 'nice girl', I was not used to upsetting people and it felt humiliating to me.

The short-term effect of his behaviour was I ended up in a sobbing heap in the toilets. Thanks to supportive colleagues, I managed to go back to my desk and put right my error. The long-term effect was that my confidence took a real knock, until I changed my perspective on the situation enough to come out of victim mode and speak up for myself.

The roots of aggressive communication are usually around a need to win or be right. You may feel criticised, defensive or totally disagree with the other person, but that doesn't mean you are entitled to ignore their opinion or idea, or be pushy, patronising or bullying. Learning to control your initial reaction and instead respond with less emotion, allows you to move from aggression to assertiveness.

The feeling of aggression is not a bad thing and comes hand in hand with aggressive thinking. Rather than turning those angry feelings against another person and being hostile or raging, use the emotion to respond positively and assertively.

Passive aggressive Communication

Have you ever been standing in a food queue, getting frustrated as the person in front is taking ages to decide what they are having? Rather than saying anything, do you try to hold back your anxious and resentful feelings, only for them to leak out in the form of eye-rolling and tutting?

This is passive aggressive communication. You are not speaking up, but your angry feelings are coming out non-verbally. People who are in a pattern of passive aggressive behaviour will not confront someone with their true feelings and on the surface appear to be agreeing. They will then store up those resentful feelings and let them out to others later, or worse, use sabotaging techniques to ensure they get even.

This style of communication is the 'I'm Not Okay, You're Not Okay' version, as you are not respecting yourself by speaking up, and the other person will very likely pick up on your unspoken resentment.

By not directly expressing their anger and instead subtly undermining someone, a passive aggressive person will:

- Deny there is a problem

- Exhibit body language and facial expression that does not match their feelings
- Appear to co-operate but do things to annoy or distract
- Feel and become alienated from those around them
- Feel stuck in a place where they are powerless

Assertive Communication

In contrast to those communication styles above, assertive communication is a win-win situation. The 'I'm Okay, You're Okay' style. If you want to maintain your relationship with the person you are speaking to, then this is by far the best way.

The principle behind assertiveness is about respecting the other person's needs and opinions as well as your own. When you show this mutual respect you're recognising that you both are of equal value and your words come from your core nugget of self-worth.

It's important to speak up not just for what you want, but also for your boundaries and beliefs.

If we don't speak up for ourselves, we assume the other person knows what we think. Instead, speaking up calmly and confidently builds an honest and open relationship.

The benefits of being assertive include:

- Building your self-confidence and self-esteem
- Helping you understand and recognise your feelings
- Earning you respect from others
- Creating win-win situations

155

- Improving your decision-making skills
- Creating honest relationships
- Providing more job satisfaction

You may feel nervous about speaking up for yourself in case you upset others. But you have no control over their reaction, and you are assuming they will be unreasonable.

An excellent example of not speaking up for what you want was Gemma. I coached Gemma through some difficult times in her work as a freelance journalist. She had been successful in her journalism career and had decided to go freelance to give her more flexibility around her family.

The problem Gemma had was that she felt uncomfortable asking for what she was worth. Gemma's feelings of not being Good Enough meant she didn't value her expertise.

When offered an assignment, she felt uncomfortable to challenge what they offered and accepted any fee they suggested. She feared upsetting people and losing the work but taking the going rate made her feel resentful.

Gemma recognised that she was damaging her career and her confidence by not speaking up and looked to me for the accountability and support to enable her to get heard.

I challenged her to ask for the fee she wanted for each assignment and to focus on asking rather than on the outcome. We took this one step at a time, gradually upping her rate and reflecting on her achievements that backed up her salary expectations.

As Gemma says, "At first I felt really uncomfortable and didn't believe I was worth it. Now I realise that by undervaluing myself, I was suggesting my work was below standard, and I know now it certainly is not."

One of the reasons many women like Gemma fail to be assertive is they don't feel they have the right to say No or to ask for what they want. To illustrate how wrong this is, I have compiled the *Bill of Assertive Rights*.

Your Bill of Assertive Rights

The following list of personal rights applies to you and everyone else and is a quote from Manuel J. Smith[xxxix].

Being assertive means asserting these rights for yourself but also acknowledging that others also have the same rights.

Remember this list isn't exhaustive, and you may want to add your own rights to it:

- I have the right to be the judge of what I do and what I think
- I have the right to offer no reasons and excuses for my behaviour
- I have the right to refuse to be responsible for finding solutions to other people's problems
- I have the right to change my mind
- I have the right to make mistakes
- I have the right to say, 'I don't know.'
- I have the right to make my own decisions
- I have the right to say, 'I don't understand.'

157

- I have the right to say, 'No' without feeling guilty
- I have the right to be miserable or cheerful
- I have the right to be illogical in my decisions
- I have the right to set my own priorities
- I have the right to be myself without having to act for other people's benefit

Some of these rights will feel very uncomfortable but reminding yourself of them will lighten your worries and boost your self-esteem.

How assertive are you? Have a go at this questionnaire to help you find out.

How Assertive Are You?

In the box, enter how comfortable you feel in each situation.
Score 1 if you feel very uncomfortable
Score 2 if you feel slightly uncomfortable
Score 3 if you feel reasonably comfortable
Score 4 if you feel very comfortable

Situation	Score 1, 2, 3 or 4
Complaining about the service you received in a restaurant or shop	
Expressing your anger to someone when you are angry	
Receiving a compliment and thanking them	

Openly discussing another person's criticism of you	
Speaking up in front of a group	
Telling a friend that they are doing something that bothers you	
Requesting the return of a borrowed item without apologising	
Initiating a conversation with a stranger	
Telling an acquaintance that you like him or her	
Returning a faulty item.	
Asking a favour of someone	
Turning down a request for a meeting or a date	
Admitting to fear or ignorance	
Asking for and accepting constructive criticism	
Saying 'No' to someone without apologising	
Arguing with another person	
Touching a colleague or friend affectionately	
Treating yourself or doing something just for you	
Refusing a friend a favour when you don't want to do it	
Telling a friend about how you're feeling inside and why	
Total Score	

Any score above 60 shows you have pretty good assertiveness skills. Be careful to ensure you're respecting others' feelings too.

If you score below 60, then it's worth looking at the types of situations you scored poorly in and set yourself goals to improve your skill.

The Four Types of Communication in Real Life

In her book, *A Woman In Your Own Right*, Anne Dickson[xl] describes the four communication styles as four different women. I have used her idea to illustrate to you the contrasting styles in action.

Let me introduce to you:

- Doormat Dawn (passive)
- Pauline-Anne (passive aggressive)
- Aggressive Amy (aggressive)
- Assertive Anna (assertive)

Imagine being in the weekly team meeting at work, and yet again, a more experienced colleague undermines your idea, either by saying it has been tried before and failed or by just immediately disagreeing.

This has happened a few times before, and you have managed to ignore it, but now it feels personal, and you want to react.

How would each of our ladies above react?

Doormat Dawn, being passive, obviously wouldn't react. She'd feel angry and humiliated but would decide it is easier not to get involved in an argument and cause conflict. That would leave her resentful, and it might knock her self-esteem as she hasn't valued herself enough to speak up against the unprofessional behaviour.

Pauline-Anne would have a similar reaction and not speak up. However, she would also roll her eyes, give looks like daggers or mutter under her breath. After the meeting, she would rant to anyone who listened about how awful her colleague was. She may even sabotage his ideas in the future to get her own back.

Aggressive Amy, as you would expect, would react before thinking and angrily defend her idea. Her behaviour and use of language would be pushy and bordering on rude. The colleague would similarly become defensive, and it could devolve into a confrontation that could do long-term damage to their relationship and the team.

Assertive Anna could react in several ways. She may prefer to deal with the issue outside of the meeting and raise it with her colleague at an appropriate time. She could deal with it directly at the time by asking to finish explaining her idea and then inviting comments. Another way to deal with them directly is to ask them to explain further the reasons they disagree and dig deeper into those reasons. If they are challenging the idea just to undermine Anna, their lack of logic will become apparent.

161

The Basics of Assertiveness

To help you get started with being assertive try following this structure, which my clients have found helpful.

1. State the facts of the situation or acknowledge the other person's opinion. By using facts that you can both agree on, it avoids conflict and the other person becoming defensive.

For example:

'We agreed this project would be completed by the end of the month...'

'I understand that you are upset about my decision...'

2. Describe how you feel or what your opinion is using 'I' statements. By using I rather than you, it avoids blame and is less accusatory.

For example:

'I'm disappointed that the project hasn't met the deadline...'

'I believe, having considered all the background and evaluation, that my decision is correct...'

3. Tell the other person what you would like to happen now. This gives clarity and respects your wants and needs.

For example:

'I'd like to understand what the issues have been that held the project back?'

'I suggest you take some time to reflect on what I've said and let's arrange another one-to-one next week.'

4. You may want to check in with them to see if they agree or offer another option. This part of the structure is discretionary.

For example:

'Do you have that information, or do you need time to look into it?'

'Do you agree?'

5. Listen and acknowledge the other person's thoughts and opinions.

The Dos and Don'ts of assertiveness

Do:

1. Listen and acknowledge the other person's point of view, whether you agree or not. Be empathic and try to understand their perspective.

2. Respect your point of view and speak up even if you fear upsetting others.

3. Speak confidently, constructively and calmly, ensuring you are using confident body language.

4. Learn to say 'No'. If it makes you feel uncomfortable practise it in a safe situation and look for a win-win scenario, if possible.

5. Keep your explanation brief and concise. Giving a list of excuses to defend why you said no dilutes the message and confuses the other person.

6. Use robust and powerful words to communicate and ensure clarity. Such as 'will' instead of 'could' and 'want' instead of 'need'.

Don't:

1. Apologise unless there is something to apologise for. 'I'm sorry but would you mind…' takes the power out of your assertive statement and makes you sound weak.

2. Blame the other person as this will lead to conflict, use I statements instead.

3. Soften the request, e.g. 'I just wondered if you'd mind…' Soft language is appropriate in a lot of situations, but not when you want to be assertive.

4. Ask for permission to say no, e.g. 'No I can't help, I hope that's okay?'

5. Think you can control the other person's reaction. If they get upset, that is outside your influence. You can only control your own emotions, so whatever happens, keep calm.

6. Feel guilty afterwards. It isn't selfish to ask for your wants and needs to be respected, especially as you are respecting theirs.

The Assertiveness Sweet Spot

Daniel Ames, a professor at Columbia Business School and author of the paper *Pushing Up to a Point: Assertiveness and Effectiveness in Leadership and Interpersonal Dynamics*[xli] said that, "There's a sweet spot for assertiveness. If you're below the range, you're not going to get your way. If you're above it, you're not getting along with others."

Walking this fine line between being too assertive and appearing aggressive and not being assertive enough and going unnoticed is yet another double bind for women. If they tip one way, they are seen as lacking confidence and competence, but going over the line, in the opposite direction, can result in being called bossy or bitchy.

Revolutionising gender stereotypes at work is a long-term solution to this issue. In the meantime, women and men need to be supportive in calling out the negative impact of women being assertive.

How do you know whether you are assertive enough or too assertive?

The simplest way is to pay attention to the response from the other person. Their body language and verbal response will tell you how effective your statement was. Another indicator is if you achieve your outcome. Otherwise you can ask for feedback from other people on your assertive style.

Client Story: Claire

If you have ever had a member of your team dismiss your authority and undermine your expertise, then you will know how Claire felt when she came to see me.

Claire was employed to work alongside a colleague, Nick, at the same level when she first joined a large engineering company. Two years later a restructure led to her promotion and the recruitment of two new team members to work with her old colleague, managed by Claire.

Claire knew it would be difficult for Nick having to report to her and hoped that their previous relationship would continue. Six months into the role however it was evident that Nick was not acknowledging Claire's seniority and would 'hold court' in team meetings, disrupting the discussion.

Claire had tried to manage the situation indirectly by having a chat with Nick but felt very uncomfortable tackling the issue directly.

From our work together, she quickly identified her behaviour as passive aggressive. She understood that there were ways she could speak to Nick directly and still maintain their relationship.

Claire worked hard at developing her assertiveness and tried out several assertive statements to get Nick on board.

'I understand that a lot has changed since the restructure and we are all settling into our roles. I am working to develop our new team members and would appreciate your support as an experienced and valued colleague, in sharing your expertise with them.'

166

Also, *'You have a lot of knowledge and experience in this department, which I value and I do consider it when I allocate projects. I need you to take responsibility for the delivery of the projects on time. Do you have any concerns about this?'*

Nick did improve but he was still affecting the team's performance. Claire realised that she needed to be increasingly direct with her assertiveness to hit the 'sweet spot' with Nick. She also needed to take ownership of her role as a manager and worry less about her previous relationship with Nick.

She found this very uncomfortable, but with support has found her own way of approaching the issues assertively.

'Since our last discussion, I have noticed that in our team meetings, your contributions tend to be negative and undermine the ideas that the others and I suggest. Is there anything concerning you that is behind these behaviours?'

Nick did acknowledge that he could be more supportive, but he didn't open up about any issues. As a result, Claire had to continue being direct in response to his performance, and eventually, Nick moved company.

Despite the outcome, the whole situation was a significant development opportunity for Claire. She found her voice and now has no concerns about speaking up to her team or the top level of the company.

Self-Coaching Activity

1. Which of the four communication styles do you predominantly use and why?

167

2. Evaluate your assertiveness using the questionnaire above. What does it tell you about the situations in which you find it easy or difficult to ask for what you want?

3. Identify a relatively safe situation where you can practise being assertive. It could be with family or trusted colleagues. Using the structure I've described have a go at speaking up for what you want or feel. Get used to hearing your voice being assertive and acknowledge your achievements.

4. Observe how people react to your assertiveness style. Have you hit the 'sweet spot'?

In A Nutshell

- The four basic styles of communication are passive, passive aggressive, aggressive and assertive. The most effective method for maintaining a good relationship and meeting both sets of needs is assertiveness.

- If you feel uncomfortable speaking up for your thoughts remember the *Bill of Assertive Rights*.

- Remember the structure of an assertive statement. Use facts, 'I' statements, keep sight of what you want and check in with the other person.

- Finding the 'assertive sweet spot' is essential for successful communication

Chapter 12

Having That Difficult Conversation and Dealing with Conflict

"Difficult conversations are almost never about getting the facts right. They are about conflicting perceptions, interpretations, and values."
Douglas Stone, _Difficult Conversations_

Have you ever lain awake at night with anxiety spinning around your head as you go over and over a conversation you need to have the next day? Me too.

Starting a conversation with someone when you believe they won't want to hear what you have to say can be extremely daunting. Imagine telling your boss the report your working on won't be ready for the deadline, or the projected sales, you had pretty much guaranteed, won't be achievable.

Having to give negative feedback to a team member, deal with bullying or announcing redundancies, are equally uncomfortable. Dealing with conflict and difficult conversations are, however, part of a leadership role and a crucial skill to learn.

The valuable lesson I've learnt about discussing contentious issues; is that it's all about emotions. The emotions involved from your side could include fear of upsetting the other person, how you feel about the subject you have to discuss and how you feel about the other person involved. From their perspective, the emotional reaction they have to what you say relates to their belief about the situation and their attitude towards you.

Being a highly empathic person, I found giving a message to someone that they wouldn't want to hear very uncomfortable. Not because of a fear that of their reaction, but from discomfort about the hurt they would feel.

I found that taking myself out of the situation and speaking as a representative of the organisation instead really worked for me. It allowed me to be professional and not procrastinate, and to deal with the issue in a fair and straight forward way.

Other ways to manage the conversation successfully are:

1. **Decide beforehand the purpose of the discussion.** What would you like the outcome to be? Bear this in mind throughout the interaction.
2. **Have a plan thought out about how you will approach the discussion.** Taking the lead is essential and will give you confidence in the direction of the debate.
3. **Consider whether you should give the other person a chance to prepare**
4. **Use a calm and assertive approach to state your point of view.** Be upfront with the issue or bad news and be concise but specific with your description.
5. **Plan how to avoid objections.** You can do this by using what Daisy Dowling in *7 Tips For Difficult Conversations*[xlii] calls an 'And Stance'. 'And I know you worked long hours on this project...' or 'And I

know you have just joined the company...'. This can avoid being distracted from the purpose of the conversation by lots of excuses or reasons.

6. **Follow this by actively listening to their reaction and views**. Summarise what you have heard to acknowledge that you have taken in their opinion, even if you don't agree with it.

7. **Remember that you cannot control their reaction.** People often have an initial emotional reaction, which feels excessive for the situation. This can be a defensive reaction, and you need to be patient and allow them the chance to offload. If they get very angry or upset, you may want to call a time out, to allow them the space to express themselves. Be empathetic for the way they feel, despite your own beliefs.

8. **Take out the personal**. I know from my own experience that this is easy for me to say and quite tricky to do. By detaching yourself from any comments and instead seeing yourself as doing your appointed role, these conversations will be better for both sides.

9. **Imagine that it is 3-months or a year from now**. This conversation will seem less important in the bigger picture.

10. **Find a resolution**. It may be that you have a particular outcome that is non-negotiable, or you might be looking to come to an agreement. Allowing exploration of all the options is the most productive way to find a compromise.

Dealing with conflict

Conflict is widespread in the workplace environment, especially when there are teams that work very closely together. The ability to recognise conflict, understand and resolve it is a great asset in a career. Taking action rather than hiding from a confrontational situation will mean you stand out from your peers.

Difficult conversations, as we discussed above, can include but are not always about conflict.

In every organisation, some people will use emotions to manipulate others or to cover up the flaws in their performance. They are very good at emotional outbursts, self-serving lies or exaggerations and blame-shifting.

Then there are the natural causes of conflict for any team such as competitiveness, jealousy, resource discrepancies and misunderstandings.

Conflict can also be a positive thing. It can create healthy debate and innovative solutions. Therefore, it is essential to determine whether the situation is negative and if it needs a resolution before jumping in.

As a leader, your role is to identify any potential negative conflict and to be proactive in preventing them.

You can do this by having clear boundaries for team discussions in place, well-defined job descriptions and agreed team behaviours. Being aware of tensions within the team and encouraging your team to be open with you will allow you to pick up on issues before they reach the conflict stage.

What can I do when conflict happens?

The critical point is to deal with negative conflict quickly, don't procrastinate or believe it will sort itself out. Take action now, or resentments will build up, and the whole team culture and output will be affected. You also risk losing your good employees if you can't maintain a healthy and safe environment.

You can manage team conflicts by facilitating the team to have an open discussion. Encourage them to ask questions and bring to the table their issues. Don't allow the discussion to get personal and blaming, instead, try to keep the focus on compromise and potential solutions.

If an individual is causing conflict within the team or with another colleague, you can have a chat with them one to one or play the mediator. Again allow both sides to air their views and look for a solution.

In some situations, a person's behaviour may be unacceptable and breach the boundaries you have for your team. In these cases, the performance management route may be the most appropriate.

Once you start listening to those involved, you are likely to find that one of the main drivers of the conflict is communication. Whether it's a lack of communication, incorrect information or misunderstood intention, I find that the lack of clear, concise and timely communication is often behind my clients' conflict challenges.

I can recall a peer of mine in the corporate world whom I didn't know very well, storming out of a meeting, shouting that they quit. Their reason was not being informed of a

173

change to management structure, at the same time as us. It was an unfortunate miscommunication by our boss and not an intentional snub. However, this example distinctly expounds the other big player in conflict - emotional reactions.

If we drive our decisions from our ego or our emotions, we can cause conflict where it wasn't necessary. In this instance, my peer did calm down and apologised. But he had broken some of the trust in him, and he changed his job not long after.

Client Story: Teresa

Teresa's story was one I hear far too often from my clients. She contacted me after dealing with a bullying situation at work for over a year. The constant undermining from her boss (who was female) had knocked her confidence and her self-worth. She was considering changing organisation but she didn't even have the self-belief to apply for jobs or to go to the interview process.

The types of behaviour Teresa's boss was displaying were ignoring her points in meetings or dismissing them abruptly, and mocking her abilities in front of others, deliberately favouring and flattering her colleagues.

Initially, Teresa felt this was just her boss's character, and she just needed to toughen up. With time though Teresa felt her mental health was suffering. She was exhausted and irritable at home and anxious at work. The quality of her work was affected, her clients were less amicable, and she was making herself invisible at work.

Teresa had discussed the issue with her peers, who had noticed the behaviour but told her to ignore it. They suggested it was just their boss's personality. Several times Teresa mentioned to her boss that she felt undermined, but she saw no change. As the months passed, Teresa felt more frustrated and demotivated and decided to approach HR. This courageous move sadly led to no action, partly due to Teresa not sharing all the evidence and her wish not to make a formal complaint.

My focus with Teresa was to protect her mental health and ensure she had support and strategies to going forward.

We then explored her options to deal with the conflict/bullying. Previously she had highlighted to her boss how she felt in passing comments. Teresa now needed to have that tough conversation with her and be explicit in her points and the outcome she wanted.

We developed a plan for the conversation that allowed Teresa to make her point and to deal with interruptions, distractions and excuses. I then asked Teresa to give her boss space to express her feelings and ask questions before she suggested a resolution for going forward.

In this situation, I'm sorry to say that her boss was shocked but didn't see Teresa's issues and didn't change her behaviour. However, Teresa was now confident enough to make a formal complaint to HR, who brought in mediation.

Since then Teresa has moved company, but she went when it was right for her, with her confidence restored and when she felt motivated to progress her career.

Self-Coaching Activity

1. What difficult conversations have you had to have in your career? Think about how you approached them and the result. Could you have done anything differently looking back?
2. Observe how other people handle those conversations, is there anything you can learn from them?
3. When you have another opportunity to start a tricky discussion re-read the 10 points above and make a plan for your interaction, rather than jumping in.
4. Do you avoid conflict? Score yourself out of 10 on how willing you are to tackle a conflict situation, where 1 is 'I always ignore it and hope it will resolve itself', and 10 is 'I always tackle conflict head on'. If you score 7 or below, what is the fear that is holding you back?

In A Nutshell

- Difficult conversations are all about emotions. Ensuring both of you get an opportunity to express your thoughts and feelings is essential to a productive outcome.
- Detaching yourself personally from the discussion and focusing on your professional role will take away some of the fear you feel.
- If you recognise conflict in your team or with others, don't procrastinate or use excuses to hide from it. Take action straight away before feelings develop further and relationships become permanently harmed.

- When you feel challenged or undermined, take a moment before reacting purely from your emotion, then get your opinion heard by speaking up assertively.

Chapter 13

Communicating with Power

"We are not here to fit in, to be well-balanced, or provide exempla for others. We are here to be eccentric, different, perhaps strange, perhaps merely to add our small piece, our little clunky, clunky selves, to the great mosaic of being. As the gods intended, we are here to become more and more ourselves."

James Hollis

Being able to communicate confidently and with authority is an essential skill in getting you to the higher levels of leadership. Developing your communication skills to deliver your message with power can be achieved by considering speech habits, body language and vocal tone.

Speech habits

Women tend to dilute the power of their message by using speech habits. This is known as minimising and can take away from the confident impression you want to achieve.

I don't want you to start beating yourself up about the way you speak, but it is worth becoming aware of these speech habits and deciding for yourself if you wish to make a change.

If you listen to a group of women talking, they will often use soft language styles such as apologising and things like, 'Would you mind?' or, 'Sorry for interrupting, but'. For women, a principal purpose of communication is to connect and build a relationship, therefore, their communication style is softer than men's who prefer to communicate for power.

There is nothing wrong with soft speech habits unless you are in a situation where you want to come across as assertive. Then softening your words will dilute or minimise your message.

Tara Mohr, in her book *Playing Big*[xliii] talks about the types of speech habits women use. Do you recognise any of them?

Hedges:

1. **Just**. 'I just wanted to ask…'; 'I just wanted to check…'. These sound apologetic and we tend to use them when we're worried about coming across too strongly. They can make you sound weak and that your point can be ignored. Whether it's in speech or an email take the word 'just' out.
2. **Just curious.** Again this is used to reassure the other person that you're not being aggressive. 'I was just curious to find out…' Remove the just curious so the message is direct and confident.
3. **Actually.** 'Actually I think…'; 'Actually I disagree…'. This is used to diminish the statement and to avoid conflict. It sounds instead like you're surprised at your thoughts and that you are unsure of what you're saying.

Apologies:

1. **Sorry, but.** By saying sorry you are apologising for speaking up or bothering someone and it automatically undermines you, so your message can be dismissed. A Canadian study by the University of Waterloo[xliv] found that women apologise more than men as they have a lower tolerance for what they count as being offensive. Try swapping the word sorry for an alternative such as, 'Could you please' or, 'Unfortunately, I'm not available'.

2. **Would you mind if** or **I know I may have this all wrong, but.** These are other versions of the apology.

3. **A little bit.** 'Can I tell you a little bit about...' this makes the person think it's not very important and not worth their time

Disclaimers:

1. **Just off the top of my head** or **I'm no expert but** or **This is just an idea.** These are all ways of diminishing your point or signalling that you haven't thought through your idea, so it could be wrong. Instead, try using, 'I think brainstorming some ideas would be helpful and here are some of mine'.

2. **Does that make sense?** This sounds like you think you've not communicated your point and may have confused them. That suggests you lack confidence. It's better to put the focus on them, such as, 'Do you have any thoughts or comments?"

Undermining habits:

1. **Uptalk.** This is when you increase the pitch at the end of a sentence, so it sounds like a question. You, therefore, give a message that you doubt or are tentative about your statement.
2. **Singsong.** This style of voice pattern swings up and down, and again diminishes the power of your comments.
3. **Rushing.** A lack of pauses or punctuations when you speak reduces the impact of your voice and is difficult to follow.
4. **Using a question, not a statement.** For example, 'Shall we take a break to reflect on this?' rather than, 'I'd like to take some time to reflect' suggests you don't have definite opinions or fear upsetting others.

Some of my clients notice these speech habits and decide immediately to work on changing them. Other clients have told me they deliberately use them to avoid sounding too direct or aggressive. For those clients, I suggest that rather than using habits that are undermining, they can find other ways to soften their language.

As Tara Mohr says, "If we're using self-deprecating speech to come across as more likeable, as we often are, we could instead try an alternative approach: conveying likeability in positive, not self-undermining ways – such as humour, making personal connections and expressing appreciation for others."

If your focus is on likeability remember that your self-worth isn't linked to how many people think you're great. As you are is Good Enough.

Body language

I have taught the benefits of a confident body language for many years, and there is an extensive amount of research on the subject. Some of the research has been spread incorrectly and is now an urban myth.

The most famous study was in the 1960s, when Professor Albert Mehrabian and colleagues at the University of California, Los Angles (UCLA) conducted studies into human communication patterns. Their abbreviated results were published in 1967, but people focused on the figures without looking at their meaning. From then onwards, the myth that communication is only 7 per cent verbal and 93 per cent non-verbal was born.

Having said that your body language and tone of voice are still a significant part of communication and can affect how confident you feel.

Think about a situation where you feel uncomfortable. It could be in a board meeting, an interview or a meeting with a crucial client. You feel nervous, anxious, and lacking in confidence. What do you imagine your body language will be like?

Unless you are consciously trying to look confident, you will likely be taking up as little space as possible, almost as if you are apologetic for being there.

You will try to shrink into yourself, crossing your arms and legs or hunching forward over the table. By doing this you are sending a message to other people that you lack confidence and don't believe in yourself.

More importantly, you are sending a negative message to yourself: 'I lack confidence' or, 'I haven't got anything worthwhile to contribute' or perhaps, 'I need to pull myself together because everyone else can do this'. These messages will further knock your confidence and self-esteem, making it more difficult to speak confidently and authentically.

You have probably heard of 'Power Poses'. They were first talked about in 2012 by Amy Cuddy in her Ted talk[xlv], following her research with colleagues at Harvard University. They tested the effect of changing from a weak to a powerful pose on levels of testosterone (confidence) and cortisol (stress levels) in participants' saliva.

They measured the levels of both hormones in the participants and then asked one group to do weak body poses, another to do power poses and a third group were the control.

What they found was that in the people doing power poses, their testosterone levels increased showing improved confidence. Their cortisol levels reduced, which demonstrated they were less stressed. In those doing weak poses, the effect was the opposite on their hormone levels. They concluded this was evidence that power poses produce confidence and soft poses create fear.

What is happening when we feel an emotion like low confidence or nervousness?

The emotion of being uncomfortable or scared is causing a change in brain chemistry, and that creates a difference in your body. In this case, your lack of belief in yourself causes you to shrink your body position physically.

This change in your body language then feeds back to the brain and reinforces to your mind that you're uncomfortable and nervous and so the cycle goes on.

It also happens with other emotions. When we're happy the chemical serotonin is released, and that has the effect on the face to make you smile.

Have a go at forcing yourself to smile now and hold it for 20 seconds... did you feel a slight uplift in your mood?

This cycle I mentioned, goes the other way too. That means if you change your body response, you can change your brain chemistry and so your mood. Using these body position tips regularly and over time will result in that confident feeling becoming regular and authentic.

Imagine you are back in that uncomfortable situation and you want to demonstrate to others and yourself that you are feeling okay and confident. How would you be sitting now?

Amy Cuddy talks about Wonder Woman poses to boost your self-belief, but that can be quite difficult in a meeting. Instead make sure your body position is open and taking up as much space as possible but is also relaxed. Make eye contact with others, show expression on your face, keep your head up and smile.

You can also use these principles when you're standing or walking. I have used the Wonder Woman power pose in the toilets before going to speak in front of large audiences. It worked for me!

Vocal tone and volume

After body language, your vocal tone, speed and volume are the other critical areas to focus on. There is nothing worse than having to listen to a dull, monotone voice, no matter how compelling their points are.

Your vocal tone needs to energetic and have a firm volume. We can never hear our voice as others do, so the only way to truly hear what you sound like is to record yourself speaking and play it back. When I suggest this to clients, there is nearly always a groan at the idea. I know it feels uncomfortable, but It is vital to help you understand your natural volume, speed and tone.

The tone of your voice communicates to the other person the attitude behind the words you're using and gives them an idea of how you are feeling. To see the impact of tone on a conversation, watch a discussion between two of your colleagues. See if you can identify their true feelings from their tone of voice, not the words.

The most important thing about tone, speed and volume are that you vary them. Increasing volume and speed as you build up to a critical point or putting in pauses to help people reflect.

Client Story: Jenny

Jenny was naturally a quiet person and had pushed herself to high standards of delivery, which meant she had a successful career in the civil service. As with many of my clients, Jenny believed that her introverted personality meant she lacked visibility at work. She recognised that, in the longer term, it would hold her career back.

Jenny's line manager and mentor had given her feedback that she lacked presence and impact in meetings. Her ideas and opinions were good, but they were often going unheard or dismissed.

I explained to Jenny that lacking presence meant that her style of communication, body language and confidence were not giving the message that she is competent and trustworthy.

Presence is challenging to define, but you know when someone has it. They get people's attention when they walk in a room. They look confident and comfortable and speak clearly and with influence over others. I'm sure you can bring to mind someone with these characteristics.

Jenny and I explored her communication style. With permission, she recorded herself in meetings and asked for 360-degree feedback from colleagues. The feedback was a real eye opener for her. To hear how her contributions lacked energy, confidence and belief, in comparison to others, gave her significant insight into what she wanted to change.

Increasing the power in your communication is a holistic approach of self-belief, language, tone, volume and body language. Jenny and I worked on all these areas. The trickiest change for her was accepting that being louder and firmer in her communication didn't mean she was arrogant or aggressive.

Jenny has done a fantastic job of boosting her visibility in meetings. She's had great feedback from her line manager, mentor and colleagues. She still isn't the loudest in the room and doesn't want to be, but she does know that she will be listened to when she has a point to make.

Self-Coaching Activity

1. Be aware of your speech; do you fall into any of the habits above? Ask for feedback from a trusted colleague or record your voice in a meeting (and yes I know how uncomfortable that can be!).

2. If stopping the use of the word sorry is tricky for you, keep count of how many times you use it in a day. When and where are you using the word? Does something or someone trigger your over-apologising? Practise replacing the word sorry with a stronger alternative.

3. Record your voice in a meeting or on the phone and consider your tone and volume. Does it have the impact and influence you would like? Play around with different volume levels and tone styles until you find one you prefer.

4. I mentioned confident body language helps you to come across assertively, so why not watch Amy Cuddy's Ted talk on the subject?[xlvi]

In A Nutshell

- Women communicate to build a relationship but this can lead to habits of softened language which minimises and dilutes your point when you want to be assertive or demonstrate confidence.
- Using apologies, diminishing phrases and questions rather than statements to avoid conflict, may keep your likeability factor high but won't deliver impact or your outcome
- Your body language not only sends a message to people around you about how confident you are, but also sends a message internally to reinforce how you feel.
- Vocal tone and volume communicates your attitude to a discussion as well as how confident you're feeling.

Chapter 14

Earn Your Value: ask for the pay rise you deserve

"When we pay women less than men, we're telling women their work isn't as valuable. We're all equally valuable. And we should be paid equally."
Maria Shriver

According to research by Mintel in 2018[xlvii], in the UK 42% of men are happy to ask for a pay rise but only 22% of women. Does that surprise you?

There are not many other issues at work that are more emotive than salary. Where your pay sits in comparison to your colleagues can have a powerful motivational or negative effect. Some companies insist that you never share your salary, and in others, employees share quite openly.

Would you want to know what your colleagues earn, and if you did, what would you do with that information?

With the requirement for companies with more than 250 employees to report their gender pay gap now, it was hoped the additional focus would lead to a reduction in the gap. In the second year of reporting, the gap has stayed about the same, with the median pay gap going down from 9.7% to 9.6%.

When I talk to my clients about how satisfied they are with their salary, about 60% are happy. The remainder feels they deserve more but believe it is not worth asking their boss. Usually, because the company has a structured salary process and unless they move grade, any request would be turned down.

I appreciate that being committed at work is not just about money. In my corporate career, I know I also wanted to feel recognised and fulfilled. Salary, however, is seen as an indicator that your work is valued.

Why do women find it hard to negotiate or ask for a pay rise?

In recent years there's been conflicting research about whether women ask for salary rises as much as men. However, whether you are male or female, several factors are affecting why we don't ask.

1.   Not negotiating your starting salary

When you are offered a contract, many women find it uncomfortable to negotiate, especially when it is your first job and the salary has been advertised. The long-term effect of this though can be huge.

Imagine you start on £45,000 and get a 1% increase every year, by your retirement age you would be earning £70,400 per year. Whereas, if you'd negotiated a £5,000 higher starting salary and every three years asked for and got a 4% increase, you would be on £121,300 per year.

The big difference is that over a working lifetime, you would have earned £1.06 million more. Wow!

When you are offered a position, check in with yourself, does this salary feel right to me for my experience and value? You can ask if there is a set starting salary for everyone and what their gender pay gap is. Asking for more will not lose you the job, instead, it shows you value yourself. Recruitment is a 2-way process.

Make sure you have taken the time to review the contract. If you have had a higher salary turned down, ask for a salary review to be written in after your probation period or in 6 months.

2. Don't assume your work will be rewarded

The belief that hard work gets its just reward is, I'm afraid, rarely the case. If you think that your boss is seeing all the work you deliver but doesn't come forward with a bonus or pay increase, then it is time for a new plan to make yourself more visible.

3. Not feeling Good Enough

As the title of this book shows, if you don't believe you are Good Enough, you are unlikely to feel you deserve a salary increase. You might know that you do a great job but not be aware of all the value you add to the business.

I hope that having read the contents of the book, you're reassured that your golden nugget of self-worth exists and that you are always enough.

4. Fear of rejection

As women, in general, we tend to worry more than men, particularly around past events and future possibilities. It is that future 'what if' worrying that can hold you back from putting in a pay rise request.

All those potential embarrassing scenarios can flood your mind. 'If they say no I'll feel unappreciated and look ungrateful to my boss. Perhaps he will think I'm full of myself?'

This kind of thinking can paralyse you into inaction, but remember that these scenarios are fiction, not reality.

5. Being seen as bossy/aggressive

This fear has some truth in reality. The Mckinsey & Co report *Women In The Workplace* written in 2018[xlviii] showed that women who negotiate a pay rise are 30% more likely to get feedback that they are aggressive or bossy than men. Yet another double-bind that affects women's likeability.

As Sheryl Sandberg, founder of *Lean In*, said in the *Wall Street Journal*, "We expect men to be assertive, look out for themselves, and lobby for more — so there's little downside when they do it. But women must be communal and collaborative, nurturing and giving, focused on the team and not themselves, lest they be viewed as self-absorbed. So when a woman advocates for herself, people often view her unfavourably."

6. Not knowing how to go about asking

When should I ask, how should I ask and what do I need to prepare? Fortunately, that is what I'm going to cover next.

Are you ready to ask for a pay rise?

Before thinking about asking for a promotion or pay rise try the checklist below.

Answer each question with a score of 1 to 5, where 1 means, I disagree completely and 5 means, I agree completely.

Question	Score
I have evidence of my achievements, feedback and contribution to the company	
I feel comfortable talking about my successes to my boss and other seniors	
I have a network of key people in all areas of the business	
My colleagues and team respect me	
I am prepared to take risks	
I know the value of my experience and potential both internally and externally	
I have achieved higher than average appraisals	
I have a senior manager who will advocate for me	
I am visible and have impact in the business	

I believe my current level of pay doesn't reflect my experience and contribution to the company	
Total Score	

How did you score? What particular areas do you need to focus on before you ask for a pay rise?

How do I prepare?

- **Find out your value**.

Investigate the value of your role, expertise and experience. You need to do this internally as well as investigating your value in the marketplace. There are a few websites that will give you salary checker information, for example Glassdoor.co.uk. Also, consider job sites that will provide you with an idea of salaries for similar roles. If you network with people holding a corresponding position, they can be helpful to give you inside information, and some professional associations do salary reviews too.

Be aware that salaries will vary according to the size of the business and location.

This information will give you an indication of your value and demonstrate to your manager the importance you place on your request.

- **Collate your evidence**.

As you would for an interview, prepare proof of your successes and contributions. The more you can quantify them, the more impact your examples will have. Focus on two or three key achievements that demonstrate the value you add and the potential you have shown. Do not overdo it; remember this is not a performance review.

- **List your extra responsibilities**.

Think about any increases in responsibility, such as more team members. Also, any special projects you have undertaken or managed.

- **Have a pay goal in mind**.

Rather than vaguely asking for a pay rise, have a definite figure in mind, but ensure that it is realistic in comparison to the research you have done. As the process is a negotiation, you may want to ask for a slightly higher figure than you are hoping for.

- **Set up a meeting with your manager**.

Ambushing your manager will make them less focused on what you have to say. They will also need time to research and discuss your request.

- **Be aware of the company's pay review process**.

Your company is likely to have a structured process with annual pay increases and bonus payments. If this exists, then you may feel it is not worth the time and effort you would need to put in for your request. I would suggest, however, that it is worth flagging to your manager how you feel and the research you have done, even if the answer is no. If you have just had a success, personally or as a team, it is an excellent opportunity to start a discussion. As is if the company announces good financial results, your contract ends, or you are asked to take on more responsibility.

Many women I have talked to tell me they get prepared to ask for an increase, but never actually do. Instead, they procrastinate and convince themselves that it's not the right time or they haven't had enough experience or other reasons.

I remember receiving a promotion at work and being told that as I was already within the pay scale for that grade, I would not get a pay increase. I was shocked at the time and didn't react. Having thought about it afterwards, I felt demotivated and undervalued. I reviewed my current role against the new one in terms of responsibility and decided that I needed to speak up against a decision that I felt was unjust.

Fairness is a core value of mine, which meant I was highly motivated to make a stand. I was still very nervous though and definitely procrastinated for a while. My manager admitted later that he was surprised by my stand, but I did get a small increase, which felt good.

Sometimes asking for a pay rise can be less about the money and instead about equality and feeling valued.

What do I say?

According to Susan Heathfield in *How To Ask For A Pay Rise*[xlix], "The negotiation for a pay rise is about asking for what you deserve based on your merits and accomplishments. A successful negotiation is never based on why you need additional money. While your employer may care about you, providing extra money to fund your chosen lifestyle is not their responsibility."

If you are considering using another job as leverage to get a pay rise, I would think twice before you decide to. It is always a gamble, and are you happy to take the new job if you don't get what you want?

Having researched and got another role, if you decided to back down and stay without extra salary, you may be seen as halfway out of the door and not get the career development or the opportunities that you could have had previously.

Do you feel nervous about asking? Then practise what you want to say, keep it concise and focus on the key reasons you believe you deserve it. Body language is essential as well to give a confident and respectful impression. Avoid shrinking into yourself, be open, make eye contact and smile.

Do not fall into the speech habits mentioned in the last chapter of apologising or softening your words; this is a time to be assertive, clear and listen.

What if they say no?

There could be any number of reasons for your request to be turned down. The company's financial situation may not be as good as you thought. Pay increases may be restricted to once a year, or your boss may not think your performance is at the level to deserve a rise.

Whatever the excuse/reason given, you still have options:

> 1. Remember this is not a rejection of you. As we have said, there are multiple reasons why you

may be turned down, and most are not about you!

2. Ask for a review in 6 months, or when the companies situation changes.

3. Ask what you would need to do to justify a pay rise and get specific objectives agreed, with a review.

4. Suggest other benefits such as working from home, flexible hours, extra holidays, professional qualification paid for etc.

5. Request additional training or mentoring

6. If none of these are an option and you feel genuinely dissatisfied, then maybe it's time to look for another job.

Always follow up with an email confirming what has been agreed and review dates.

Client Story: Amy

I was asked by a financial organisation to come in and coach one of their senior leaders, Amy. The company saw her as having potential, but I was told her relationship with her boss was very difficult. And they believed that this was holding her career back.

Having spoken to Amy, she agreed that she was being held back from getting a pay rise and promotion by her boss and felt frustrated and undervalued as a result.

I asked Amy if she had ever asked her boss for a salary increase and expressed how she felt? She had, but from Amy's explanation of their salary discussion, I could see that they had clashed. She had been refused, which had further added to their unhealthy working relationship.

I began exploring how Amy and her boss interacted and communicated, what Amy believed were her boss's priorities, perspective on the business and expectations of her. With time Amy began to recognise how miscommunication and different personality styles had fanned the flames of their resentment.

Amy could now see that a lot of the issues and disagreements were in her head.

Having a totally different mindset enabled Amy to find a way of working with her boss and demonstrating the value she brought to the business above her colleagues. Their relationship is far from perfect, but there is now some mutual respect.

Amy finally felt ready to ask for a pay rise again, and she put in place all the preparation necessary and confidently put over her case. The answer was YES! I heard from her 6 months later - she has also got the promotion she hoped for.

Self-Coaching Activity

1. What is your money mindset? The messages we pick up as children about money can become beliefs later in life, reflect on what yours could be.
2. Try this exercise – visualise your annual salary, now imagine if you earned that every month, wow! Do you think that is possible? Write down all the reasons you don't believe it is possible. These are your limiting beliefs about money.

3. Have you ever asked for a pay rise? If not, what is your fear? Is that a genuine worry or an insecure excuse? If you knew you would be okay whatever the result was, would you ask?

In A Nutshell

- Research by Mintel in 2018 showed that in the UK 42% of men are happy to ask for a pay rise but only 22% of women.
- The most critical time to negotiate a pay rise is when you start a job, especially your first one. You could be a million pounds better off when you retire if you do.
- Ensure you prepare fully before speaking to your boss. Know your value, have evidence of your achievements and extra responsibilities.
- Ask confidently, concisely and with clarity.
- If you get a no, ask for feedback and other benefits.
- **Just Ask!**

Chapter 15

Work the Room – A Modern Woman's Guide to Face-to-Face Networking

"Networking is all about connecting with people. But then again, isn't that what life is about?"
Jay Samit

One of women's strongest traits is the ability to connect with others using their emotional intelligence. Therefore, you might think they would be excellent networkers. Many women are, but for others, either they feel uncomfortable doing it or they are not maximising the opportunities it offers.

Undervaluing networking can have a significant impact on your career progression. People who network have greater access to resources, information, opportunities and support. The benefits of this include learning, recommendations for new roles, innovation and higher authority and status.

Why do I need to network?

- A survey in 2016 by Lou Sadler of Performance-Based Hiring[1] showed that 85% of jobs are filled by networking of some sort.
- Other experts say that between 60 and 80% of people have found a job through networking.

- According to interviewsuccessformula.com[li], up to 80% of posts are never even advertised. Instead, they are filled internally or by connections recommended and known through networking.

If that doesn't persuade you, then another survey by LinkedIn[lii], showed that almost 80% of professionals consider professional networking to be essential to career success.

The message from this is that if you are looking for a new position, then networking is essential. Having a diverse network will ensure you know about possible opportunities, as only 20% of jobs are advertised.

> *Even if you aren't looking for a new role, building connections who trust you and would recommend you in the future is still critical.*

What stops me from networking?

A lot of people hate networking, as they say it feels uncomfortable, manipulative and fake. Those who do love it tend to be the extroverts who thrive on social interactions and making conversation.

I networked face to face, both as part of my corporate career and when starting up my business. I generally found it comfortable, but I am not sure how effectively I made use of the events.

In my own business, I used networking as a way of demonstrating my expertise and authority. Like many people, I did tend to spend time with people I already knew, or with whom I felt a connection.

The key issues I hear that stop women networking are:

1. Lack of time

Nearly half of all professionals, while saying how vital networking is, don't regularly keep up with their network or attend events. Lacking time is quoted as the main reason for this, however the most successful professionals are the ones who see networking as a priority within their role.

2. The wrong motivation

Clients of mine who struggle with networking say they do it to tick the box. Networking from this place is always going to feel uncomfortable and be ineffective. Instead, be curious about other people and companies and see it as an opportunity to learn

3. I hate small talk

A lot of women who categorise themselves as introverts have a fear of small talk. They put an enormous amount of pressure on themselves to be interesting and entertaining. The result of that is they are so up in their heads with whirling worries that they have nothing to say. Take the pressure off yourself and remember a conversation takes two people.

4. It's manipulative and inauthentic

I can understand why women feel like this, as networking can mean only seeing people at a superficial level and their 'best self'. It doesn't have to be like this though, the more authentic and open you are, the more people will warm to you and relax.

5. Family commitments

A lot of women still carry the significant share of caregiving for the family. As a result networking activities after work can be impractical or women may decide they are less important than family commitments.

How to love and be productive at networking

According to Caroline Castrillon in *Why Women Need to Network Differently*[liii], men and women have contrasting network styles, and that is not necessarily a bad thing. Men tend to focus on the short term, have a clear goal in mind and ask for what they want. As Rachel Thomas, president of *Lean In*, says, "I think men are socialised from the get-go to understand that mixing business and friendship is what you do to get ahead. We, as women, aren't as comfortable doing that."

Men also have a higher likelihood of connecting with someone that can help their career as they tend to have larger and broader networks.

Women, in contrast, prefer to build long-term connections or friendships with fewer people, but a deeper level of trust. They are less likely to ask for what they want in a networking situation and instead focus on what they can do to support the other person.

This tight network of fabulous women is a vital support in discussing professional and personal challenges as well as flagging job opportunities. A study conducted by the Kellogg School of Management said, "A network's gender composition and communication pattern predict women's leadership success"[liv]. They found that women with a tight female inner circle were three times more likely to get a job than those with a male-dominated network or no support system.

The answer to improved networking for women is not to be false and try to network like a man would but instead as Tiziana Casciaro says in her article *Learn to Love Networking*[lv] keep the focus on what you want out of networking and build deeper relationships.

So how do you ensure you can enjoy and get the most out of networking?

1. Approach networking with openness and curiosity

Rather than seeing networking as a 'necessary evil' choose a different mindset. See the possibilities to learn more about people and have an exciting conversation that might open up new opportunities. When you are in this frame of mind, you are likely to be warm and authentic, which people will pick up on.

2. Have a purpose

If you see the benefit of networking as only self-promotion or for your career development it can seem less important. Having a collective goal, like ensuring women's voices are heard in a male-dominated environment or gaining knowledge to help clients, makes the purpose feel motivational.

3. Think about what you have to offer

If you are a senior person networking with juniors, then it can seem obvious what you have to offer: experience, influence, knowledge. As a result, networking can be a lot easier as you know what you have to give.

What if you are junior to other networkers or they are your peers, what value do you have to add then?

Don't consider just the obvious resources, which may be limited in a junior role. Think about people you can connect with as they have common interests. Share gratitude for the inspiration of a role model or your perspective of a company or industry, which will come from a different place to a senior leader.

Knowing you have something new to offer to a networking situation can help you feel comfortable and of value.

4. Develop an elevator pitch

An elevator pitch is a quick and inspiring description of what you or your organisation's purpose is.

Imagine being at a networking event, and someone turns to you and asks, 'What do you do?' Does your mind go blank and you stumble over a few thrown together words? Or do you announce your job title: 'I'm a systems analyst', and the other person looks blankly at you?

Your elevator pitch is that pre-prepared response to the question, that gives a nugget of information about your role while piquing their interest to ask you more.

What to remember about an elevator pitch:

- **It's not a sales pitch**. Unless you are specifically in a sales situation, then an elevator pitch is an opportunity to engage the other person/people in a conversation and build a connection.
- **It is a two-way communication**. The best elevator pitches result in a two-way conversation, where the other person is relaxed and interested. To give the other person something to ask about, include a hook in your words.
- **Keep it short**. Keep your pitch to about 20 seconds, if you're in a conversation after this, then that's great, and you can naturally reveal more.
- **Don't assume**. Avoid using jargon or industry speak which the other person may not understand.
- **Personal brand**. Your elevator pitch needs to be authentic, honest and congruent with your personal brand.
- **Practise makes perfect.** For your words to sound sincere, it is important to practise saying it out loud until you feel comfortable.

How to structure it:

There are a vast number of examples and templates for elevator pitches online. I like these:

SIR:

- Situation – describe the pain your clients are in
- Impact – how does this affect them, profits or sales
- Resolution – explain how you solve the problem

For example, some professional women struggle with being visible and speaking up at work, which can hold them back in fulfilling their career goals. I empower them to change their mindset and give them the skills to achieve their potential.

WOW, HOW, NOW:

- WOW – say something surprising or different that sparks the other person's interest
- HOW – answer the probably unspoken question, 'What does that mean' and explain what you do
- NOW – give an example in a storytelling way

I open doors for professional women by empowering them to overcome their self-doubts and achieve their career potential. I've recently worked with a client who ... and as a result they...

208

The Four Types of Networkers

Before discussing practical tips on how to network, let me introduce you to four ladies and their networking style.

1. Loner Lisa

Lisa works in insurance; she hates networking and avoids it if she can. If she is asked to go, she will arrive late and not approach anyone or join a new group. She is okay talking one-to-one but can be self-conscious and put herself under pressure to make interesting conversation. This results in her spending a lot of the time with 'shoulds' and worries rather than being present to the conversation.

Tip for Lisa: take the pressure off herself to perform and set a simple intention or goal for a networking event. Then listen actively to keep in the moment, rather than thinking about what she is going to say next.

2. Butterfly Beatrice

The opposite extreme is Beatrice, who works in the head office of an aviation company. Beatrice knows most people in her area of the industry and is recognised by them. At networking meetings, she moves quickly amongst people and groups, acknowledging everyone.

She enjoys being known and liked but doesn't spend much time with individuals, so her connections are shallow.

Tips for Beatrice: spend more time with individual connections to understand what is important to them, any common interests and to develop trust. She can use the fact she knows so many people to introduce and connect others.

3. Seller Susie

Susie is a solicitor who networks a lot, looking for new clients in her specialist area. Before the meeting, she identifies those people she wants to target. She focuses in on them straight away and is confident at small talk and approaching people.

Susie falls down on the fact that she doesn't listen well or give the connection enough time to talk and feel part of the conversation. Instead, she sells herself and her company in a way that can feel overwhelming and pressurised to many people.

Tips for Susie: if Susie paid more attention to her connections' interests and needs, she would be more likely to sell. Rather than pushing what she offers too actively, she could think about links and referrals as well.

4. Rapport Ruth

As a senior NHS manager Ruth networks internally in the NHS and externally in professional associations. She is excellent at relationship building and actively listens to the people she meets. Her extensive network allows her to introduce, connect and refer people to each other and adds value to any networking event.

Sometimes Ruth can forget to talk about herself, her wants and what she has to offer.

Tips for Ruth: ensure that she gets value out of networking by asking others for the introductions she would like and being clear on any support she would value.

Do you recognise yourself or others in these descriptions?

My top 20 networking tips

The networking style you choose to use depends a lot on your authentic approach as well as what you want to achieve from networking.

I have collated below some of my tips on networking. Not all of them will apply to you but you can use them to reflect on your approach at networking events.

1. Check the list of those attending before the event and decide who would be interesting to talk to and a useful connection. Industry leaders and influential people or their connections are obvious choices.

2. Prepare an elevator pitch that is appropriate to the situation.

3. Set your intention for the event. Do you want to speak to a particular person or to make 2 or 3 new connections or do you have a different goal?

4. Arrive on time or early, avoid the temptation to be late. Entering a room full of groups of people already in conversation can be intimidating. You may find it easier to chat to people as they arrive.

5. Although you want to make a good impression, do be yourself. It is you that connections will be referring and you can't build genuine relationships if you aren't yourself.

211

6. Research has shown that demonstrating a confident body language not only gives a competent impression to others but also affects your brain chemistry to feel confident. When you stand tall and grounded with an open body language, make eye contact and smile, it builds trust with the other person. It also affects your brain chemistry by increasing your testosterone (the hormone related to confidence). Reducing your cortisol (the hormone related to stress), and you will genuinely feel a boost in your confidence.

7. Before entering a room, a lot of people find visualising themselves full of passion and energy allows them to override any nerves. I know that if I feel low on energy or uncomfortable, I picture a friend of mine who is always upbeat, gregarious and lively. I imagine how she would enter the room and transfer that feeling to my behaviour. It works for me, so why not give it a try.

8. Avoid sticking to people you know and like already. Although this might feel comfortable and enjoyable, it isn't achieving your goal. Again setting an intention for the meeting will help you with this.

9. Don't be afraid to join a group. That is the purpose of networking: to meet new people, build new relationships and learn further information. A simple, 'Is it okay if I join you?' is polite and I have never heard anyone get a 'No!' Once you have joined the group, it is not your responsibility to make the

conversation. Listen. If they were mid-conversation, then add to it or ask a question for understanding. If the discussion has stopped, you might want to ask a question about the others, but don't be put off by feeling the pressure to start an interesting conversation.

10. Ditch the sales pitch. Although networking can be about getting new clients or business as with Susie the Seller, don't make it your only focus. Listening is the most critical skill in networking.

11. When you meet someone new, think about any possible links or referrals you could make to help them. Would they like an introduction to someone you know or could your organisation be helpful to a part of their company?

12. Rather than being seen as a seller, share a story that promotes your successes and demonstrates the passion you have for your industry. As I shared in Chapter 10 'The Art of Self-Promotion' - talking about facts and evidence of your success is not bragging. If you also bring in your team and make it an exciting story, it's a great way of explaining what you do and promoting yourself.

13. Listen actively to the other person. That means paying real attention to their body language, the words they use and being present in the moment, not up in your head thinking about yourself. You do need to share the responsibility for the conversation, but

sometimes it just doesn't flow, and it is fine to make a reason to leave it.

14. Be genuinely interested in the person, ask questions to understand what they offer and what support they would like. Questions will also allow you to discover any common interests to develop trust.

15. A great way of making contact with people who you feel could be vital to you, is to find out who in the room knows them and ask for an introduction.

16. As I have said before, don't stick to one person or group. Mingle but focus on building genuine relationships rather than working the whole room.

17. Be prepared to ask for what you want. If you would like to meet up for a coffee or to be introduced to someone in their firm, find a comfortable way to ask them.

18. Make sure you always follow up new contacts straight afterwards, whether it is to say nice to meet you or with referrals or advice etc. If they gave you a recommendation or advice, let them know what came of it.

19. Don't overpromise. For example, don't arrange to meet up if you don't intend to, or say you'll refer them and then forget. If you make a valuable connection, follow up and get a second date.

20. Plan future networking events into your diary, just doing an odd meeting every couple of months won't build that all-important network and community.

Client Story: Suzanne

Suzanne has a role in Learning and Development for a large organisation. She is successful in her career and is looking to make the step up to Head of Learning and Development. The position in her current company is unlikely to be available in the next few years, so Suzanne is investigating external roles.

We discussed her experience and how visible she is externally to her company. Suzanne told me she would describe herself as invisible, as she did very little networking and did not have a support group within the profession. This meant she was not getting to hear about potential opportunities that would be of interest to her.

As part of a campaign to build her community and raise her profile, we devised a networking strategy, identifying the most likely groups and events where she would meet people that could help progress her job search. The groups included other learning and development professionals and networks that representatives of the type of company and industry she would like to work in attended.

Although Suzanne's purpose at these events was ultimately to find a new position, her approach still had to be about forming relationships and offering value to others. Once she had built trust, she could talk about the type of role she was looking for and ask for help in her search.

Suzanne felt uncomfortable in networking situations as she'd had a bad experience of being a wallflower in the past. I worked with her on developing her small talk, being comfortable to approach groups and focusing on the other person. The most significant step forward she made was when she recognised that her inner critic was not real and did not need to be believed. This realisation that her negative voice was just a thought, freed her to ignore it and stay present instead.

Three months after we finished working together, Suzanne successfully interviewed for a Head of Learning and Development role, a position she heard about from a fellow professional she met networking.

Don't hold yourself back from being visible. Make the time to build relationships, and you could have success like Suzanne.

Self-Coaching Activity

1. How often do you attend a networking event? There is no ideal figure as it varies by industry and role, but I can be almost 100% sure you could do more.
2. Research network meetings, professional conferences, association events, meetups etc. for those that appeal to you and will raise your profile. Talk to colleagues and friends about the networking they do.
3. Put together a networking strategy for the year. Which events are you going to attend and how often? Try out different combinations of women-only and mixed-gender, professional and business, regular and one-offs. Review your strategy every quarter.

Are you getting value from attending? What else could you try?

4. Have a clear intention for any meeting you go to and reflect afterwards on what you did well and whether the situation met your needs.

In A Nutshell

- 85% of jobs are filled by networking, and only 20% of posts are ever advertised. To be aware of the opportunities out there, you need to network.
- Rather than avoiding networking, choose a new mindset of openness and curiosity. Find a purpose that motivates you and think about all the value you can add.
- When you are at networking events, ensure you listen and ask questions to find common interests as well as being open about the support you would like.
- Link and refer people, instead of selling. Building a below surface relationship with two or three others is more important than working the room.

Chapter 16

Bouncing Back: How to develop your strength and resilience

"The oak fought the wind and was broken, the willow bent when it must and survived."
Robert Jordan

Carina asked me to help her with her anxiety about failing in her new role. She had been in her new position in an engineering corporation for 6-months and felt she wasn't delivering at the strategic level that she should be. This was causing her to worry that her boss would recognise her flaws, and she might ultimately lose her job.

Having transferred to the UK from Spain two years ago, Carina had been through some tough times at work and home. Shortly after moving here with her husband, her mother had become very ill and died 6-months later. Carina had travelled back and forth between Spain and England while trying to deliver her new role effectively.

She had also found the cultural differences between workplace cultures in the two countries trickier than she expected. Her naturally direct way of approaching people had caused conflict with some colleagues and meant her working relationships were strained.

Three months after her mum died, one of her team put in a complaint about bullying against her. At the same time, Carina had to implement salary cost cuts in her area of the business.

All of this had a powerful effect on Carina's self-confidence and motivation. She decided to leave the company and find a new position. She came to me as the new role was not working out the way she had hoped and Carina recognised she needed help.

In our first conversation, I picked up that Carina still held a lot of anger and frustration about how things had worked out in the previous company. These feelings were causing her to be resistant to making decisions, taking risks and trusting herself in her new role.

When we have had a bad experience like Carina, having the courage and confidence to bounce back and 'put ourselves out there again' can feel very scary. Having the resilience and mental toughness to do that is a skill worth developing.

What is resilience?

You might think that resilience is something you are born with, a personality trait, but it's something you can learn and build over time.

Resilience is defined as the capacity to recover from difficulties. Although it is referred to as 'bouncing back' often it feels more like a battle than a simple bounce.

The foundation to resilience is in knowing you are Good Enough and recognising your golden nugget of worth and value.

According to the research of leading psychologist, Susan Kobasa, three elements are essential to resilience. These are:

1. Challenge. Resilient people see difficulty as a challenge rather than something that overwhelms them and stops them from taking action. They use problems as opportunities to develop and learn instead of taking them as a negative reflection of their self-worth or confidence.

2. Commitment. Committing to their goals in life and work means that resilient people can accept that challenges are part of their journey. By keeping their focus on the endpoint they remain motivated to carry on towards their purpose.

3. Personal Control. Resilient people put their time and effort into issues they have control or influence over. As they can have an impact on these problems, they remain confident, in contrast to worrying about uncontrollable situations which would leave them feeling powerless.

At work, you will probably notice that people have very different reactions to pressurised and stressful situations. It's interesting to observe those people that remain outwardly positive and those that struggle to keep focused and motivated.

The situations Carina found herself dealing with were very stressful, but your issue is valid no matter what you are trying to cope with. There isn't a rule that says unless your difficulty is a specific size, you have no right to complain. I've heard clients say, 'but no one died...' or, 'it wasn't an important problem...'. If it is tricky for you, then it will be genuinely stressful.

How do you build resilience?

For Carina to build her resilience, I first needed to work with her to unpack the emotions she was carrying. We then looked at the fears she had that made her resistant to being all out in her job.

To support her in developing her resilience for future situations, we worked on several strategies from this list:

1. **Reflect on your past resilience.**

when have you previously had to deal with a difficult problem at work? How did you manage it, and what did you learn?

Although Carina had struggled and felt she hadn't managed things well in her previous job, There were also positives and lessons to be taken from her experience. She recognised that there hadn't been supportive people in the company she could turn to. Something she decided to change in her new organisation. Despite everything that had happened, Carina had continued to deliver the basics of her role and to work hard., which she could now see as real strength.

2. Know your strengths and use them.

Identify what you know to be the skills and behaviours you are strong in. When things are difficult, consider how you can use those strengths to cope with the problem.

Carina had strengths around her work ethic, her technical knowledge and her problem-solving abilities. We discussed how she could specifically use these in any future situations, rather than letting the issue overwhelm her emotionally. She recognised that if she stepped away from it and analysed it as a problem instead, her natural ability would find her a solution.

3. Prioritise the things you can control.

As I mentioned before, worrying about what you can't control will only make you feel powerless. Focus on those things you *can* influence.

In Carina's case, she had no power over the decision to implement salary cost savings and make redundancies. She did, however, have influence on how she communicated the changes and the way that she dealt with her team. By keeping her attention on her circle of influence, she would have felt some level of control.

4. Build strong and supportive relationships.

If things become difficult in the workplace, it's vital to have a supportive community or individual you can rely on. They don't have to be in your organisation and can be online, but prioritising building a support network will benefit you in the longer term.

This was something Carina had failed to do in her past roles and was a goal she agreed to set herself straight away in the new company. Starting to build a network after 6 months in a company is more complicated than when you are new, and everyone is open to meet you and find out more. Carina was very courageous though and worked at it a small step at a time.

5.   Practise commitment and dedication.

When you are committed to a project or goal, it means remaining dedicated through any problems that come up. If you develop that commitment with goals you're currently working on, when a problem with a long-term project or issue develops, you will have built your resilience already.

Carina's self-doubts in her current role were stopping her from being dedicated and committed. When she understood that this was essential for building her resilience, she began to step out of her comfort zone and feel empowered.

6.   Embrace change.

The reality is that in today's workplace, change is continually happening. Whether it's mergers or restructures, projects getting cancelled, or clients changing their minds, you need to be flexible to life's surprises. Although plans changing or being completely dropped is frustrating, keeping a positive outlook to the future will help you bounce back. You can practise this both in and outside of work, by developing patience, understanding and reflecting on when you have previously shown resilience.

For Carina, it was not as much about her plans being changed by her negative experience in her first UK company, more her expectation or dream of what life in the UK with her husband and the new job would be like. She had imagined an exciting new role with great support and being recognised and valued for her successes. The different outcome was a shock and took her a long time to come to terms with.

7. **Practise self-care.**

By self-care, I mean looking after your emotional and physical self as a priority. It might be about your sleep, your diet, 'me time' or diving into your hobbies to give you some time away from your stresses. What small changes can you put in place to show yourself care?

Client Story: Carina continued

Once Carina let go of the anger about what happened and the loss of the dream she had expected in the UK, she felt ready to look at her behaviours in the new company.

We realised that her resistance to becoming visible in the company was related to her fear of 'failing' again. Reframing her previous job experience helped her understand she hadn't failed but had been in an awkward position with a lot of stresses all at once.

I then suggested Carina find clarity on precisely what was expected of her in terms of behaviours and objectives in her new role. We chunked these down into smaller goals that enabled her to see a plan for delivering her job at a higher level.

As Carina progressed with these actions, we worked on her resilience by using the strategies above. By the end of the programme, Carina had received feedback on how well she was performing. Although there had been minor setbacks at work, none of them had knocked her confidence.

Self-Coaching Activity

1. Think about what types of events in the workplace have been the most stressful for you. How have those situations typically affected you?
2. Now think about how you managed to overcome or get through those situations.
3. Do you practise self-care? Decide on three actions you are going to commit to regularly doing that are caring towards your physical and emotional wellbeing.
4. Consider the strategies above and choose two that you commit to working on to develop your resilience.

In A Nutshell

- Resilience is defined as the capacity to recover from difficulties. It is a skill you can learn rather than a personality trait you are born with.
- There are three elements to resilience: 1) Challenge – seeing difficulties as challenges. 2) Commitment – commitment and dedication to your goals. 3) Personal Control – focusing on the things you have control and influence over.

- Building a supportive network at work and practising self-care are two of the most essential strategies to building resilience.

Finally: I Am Good Enough!

"I Am Enough

I Have Always Been Enough

I Always Will Be Enough."

Reese Evans

I love this metaphor by Meir Kay which you can find on YouTube[lvi]. In it, he shows a twenty-dollar bill to a group of students and asks who wants it. They all respond, 'I do'. He then crumples it in his hand and asks who still wants it. Again they all say, 'I do'. Finally, he drops it on the floor and grinds it into the ground with the heel of his shoe, again asking who wants it now. They all still respond with, 'I do'.

Meir then says, "I have just showed you a very important lesson. No matter what I did with this money you still wanted it because it never lost its worth. It's still worth twenty dollars. There are many times in our lives when we feel like life has crumpled us up and ground us into the dirt. We may make some bad decisions or have to deal with some poor circumstances, and sometimes ... life can make us feel worthless, but no matter what has happened, no matter what will happen, you never lose your worth. You never lose your value. Never forget that."

In chapter one, I talked about self-worth being like a golden nugget that exists at our core and is always available to connect with. When we measure our worth by external things such as money, appearance, job title, who you know or what you achieve, we distance ourselves from our self-worth and are left needing more in order to feel Good Enough.

> *When you recognise your inner worth is a constant, you can accept your imperfect self and feel the security of knowing your golden nugget is always there, whatever circumstances happen in your life.*

What does self-worth look like?

Here is an example of what someone with genuine self-worth might look like:

Francesca is a mother of twins. They aren't the most academic children but do okay and are polite and kind. She works in marketing and is very good at her job. If you asked her though, she would probably say that she has a colleague who is fantastic in his role and who has a higher potential than her. Despite not being the best at her job or her children having the highest exam results; Francesca still feels pretty good about herself. She knows that being good at her job and her kids being happy is more important than being the best.

Francesca's husband works in marketing too and they are in a secure financial situation. Extras such as holidays and new cars are often out of reach, and seeing her friends being able to do things they can't afford sometimes gets to her. But she knows that money has nothing to do with her value or worth as a person and that she's still worthy of happiness, fulfilment and love.

When I think about myself, I know I have a good lifestyle. Would I want more? Of course. Would I like to change some of the things I have done or have happened to me? Definitely. Am I the kindest, best-looking, fittest, best coach and highest achieving entrepreneur I know? Absolutely not (well not always anyway!). I have flaws that I wish I didn't, like being drawn to food and wine when I'm down, a lack of patience at home or frustration when people don't see things the same way as me. But despite this I know I am a worthy person, doing my best.

You can see from Francesca and from me, that we have a wide range of abilities and we get a wide range of results from our efforts. What we recognise, most of the time, is that we are not just what we do and we can maintain the belief in our value.

You might be thinking, 'Well, of course I know that's true, but sometimes it just doesn't feel like that', and you would be right.

There are times when our thinking is negative and brings with it feelings of envy, resentment, frustration, self-doubt and sadness. These thoughts and emotions appear to be incredibly real and can trick us into not feeling Good Enough.

However, they aren't real, they are made up by our thinking, and we need to remind ourselves that at our core we are enough. Our golden nugget of self-worth is still there and ready for us to connect with.

How do I know if I'm connected to my self-worth?

I have seen many different ways of measuring self-worth in the research and work I do. This exercise is one of the simplest but most effective I have found. It was from an article by Courtney Ackerman called *What Is Self-Worth and How Do We Increase It?*[lvii]

The exercise is a list of fifteen statements and for each one you need to rate your belief on a scale from 0 (not at all) to 5 (totally or completely). The statements are:

1. I believe in myself;
2. I am just as valuable as other people;
3. I would rather be me than someone else;
4. I am proud of my accomplishments;
5. I feel good when I get compliments;
6. I can handle criticism;
7. I am good at solving problems;
8. I love trying new things;
9. I respect myself;
10. I like the way I look;
11. I love myself even when others reject me;
12. I know my positive qualities;
13. I focus on my successes and not my failures;
14. I'm not afraid to make mistakes;
15. I am happy to be me.

Add up all of the ratings for these 15 statements to get your total score. Then, ask yourself, 'What would need to change for me to improve my score ?' (For example, if you scored yourself 45 in total what would need to happen for you to move up to a 50?), then reflect on what action you can take to make that change.

How can you connect with your self-worth?

I find I'm most connected to my self-worth and happy with who I am when my mind is quiet and I am present in the moment. It can be when I'm chatting with friends, out on a walk with the family or in-flow writing this book.

Think about the times when you feel good about yourself, whatever the circumstances are. How would you describe the physical and emotional feelings to another person? Can you hang on to that feeling and can you recall it when you want to?

At that moment you are connected to your self-worth, take notice and remember how you felt. I have found the more I am aware of and recognise this feeling, the more often I return to it.

As humans, our thinking naturally takes us away from our self-worth and confidence at times. It distracts us with worry, fear or just day to day living. The trick is to realise that none of this thinking is real.

There are several behaviours that will take you away from your connection with your sense of worth. For example:

- **Worrying what others think**

If your worth and value are dependent on other people's opinions, you will never get enough approval or praise to feel good about yourself. You have no control over what they think of you, and it is unlikely that you will ever know what they genuinely believe anyway.

Of course we want to be liked and respected and to feel we fit in, but that should be a bonus on top of our self-acceptance, not the foundation of it.

The #MeToo movement has shown the shift in women's perspective from not believing they will be listened to, to valuing themselves and not worrying what others think. Having the courage to call out these unacceptable behaviours will be a powerful reconnection for these women with their golden nugget of self-worth.

The more you worry about how others perceive you, the likelier you are to do things just to please them, rather than what is right for you.

"If you find yourself constantly trying to prove your worth to someone, you have already forgotten your value." (Author unknown).

- **Believing what you do is who you are**

How do you answer the question, 'And what do you do?' Is it with your job title or the fact you are a mother or a description of exactly how you spend your time? What if the question was, 'And who are you?' How would you answer it then?

Knowing the difference between who you are and what you do is essential to feeling worthy enough. If you tie your value to your job title, what happens if the company restructures, your health suffers or you get made redundant?

- **Focusing on your appearance**

For many women, the link between how they look and how they feel about themselves is powerful. You only have to look at the eating disorder statistics to see that.

With marketing strategies and media focus on having the 'perfect' body, it's not surprising we have impossible expectations of how we should look. For those that feel their body image isn't Good Enough, it can be a constant battle, all of which gets in the way of accepting yourself as you are.

- **Always wanting more**

You probably know someone who regularly buys luxury items to prove their worth, even if it means going into debt. This continual need for more and more to fit in or to demonstrate they are better than others, can only cause a backlash to their sense of worth.

Clients I have worked with who have this behaviour find they value themselves even less the more they get. It makes them think things like, 'Even though I've got all this stuff, I'm still not Good Enough – what is wrong with me?'

If these are the thought patterns and behaviours to avoid engaging with, what can you do to feel closer to your self-worth?

These four steps will put you in a place of quiet, calm and positivity, where it is easier to reach the feeling of value and worth.

Step 1: Self-Awareness

Ask yourself these questions:

- Who am I?
- How do I see myself?
- If everything was taken away from me, how would I feel?
- What would I have left of value?
- Would I recognise my worth still?

We rarely take time to think about ourselves like this, preferring to focus on the external or top layers of our personality instead. When you do reflect on the idea of who you are and your value, it can be incredibly positive and comforting.

Step 2: Self-Acceptance

Knowing our weaknesses and flaws is something that generally we are much better at. When I ask clients to list their strengths and then their weaknesses, it's always the weaknesses that are easier.

To be human is, by definition, to be flawed, so why we are surprised or ashamed of these imperfections doesn't make sense to me.

Accepting you have made mistakes and bad decisions and forgiving yourself is often tricky. However, when you see that they have no reflection on your worth, it will be a huge step forward.

As Adam Sicinski said in *How to Build Self-Worth*[lviii], "Fully accepting yourself in spite of all your flaws, weaknesses and limitations is absolutely critical for developing a high level of self-worth."

Step 3: Self-Trust

Do you trust that if everyone you know let you down and left you alone, you would have the strength and capability to survive?

Knowing you can rely on yourself to be Good Enough, not perfect, but be Good Enough in any situation gives you a great sense of security.

You will make mistakes and wrong decisions, but if you know and accept that, ultimately you can trust your wisdom/gut intuition or whatever you want to call it. Then life will not be as scary.

To learn the behaviour of self-trust, focus on keeping promises to yourself, putting boundaries in place and listening to what you really want.

Step 4: Self-Compassion

Now you have accepted your flaws and can trust yourself, you can move on to self-compassion.

Self-compassion means treating yourself as you would a close friend that you care about, behaving towards yourself with compassion, generosity, tolerance and kindness, and seeing that you are special and unique and deserve to be treated with love, respect and encouragement, rather than berated or blamed.

Kirsten Neff PhD, who has famously written a book on self-compassion[lix], says self-compassion has three elements:

1. Self-kindness – being kind to yourself rather than self-critical or judgemental.
2. Common humanity – recognising that you are not on your own with feeling imperfect or struggling.
3. Mindfulness – balancing your reaction to emotions and seeing them as part of the bigger perspective.

I suggest you become curious about the way you behave towards yourself. Once you are aware of when you are kind and when you are cruel, you can make changes. As one of my clients said to me, "Understanding the link between my self-worth and how I treat myself was life-changing for me."

In conclusion

Throughout this book, I've talked about not feeling Good Enough. But what does being Good Enough actually mean? Good Enough for what or for whom? Against whose rules are we measuring ourselves?

Deep down, I think we all know it's not about external circumstances or what society, family or friends expect. This idea that we have to achieve or be something to be Good Enough is crazy.

Decide for yourself to break free of the idea that anyone can be *not* Good Enough. We all get to the end of most days feeling we could have achieved more, done better or been kinder. That doesn't mean we are not Good Enough.

We were born Good Enough and always will be Good Enough. My wish for you is that you see that for yourself, because then you will set yourself free.

References

Introduction

[i] Lean In: Women, Work and the Will to Lead by Sheryl Sandberg. Published in August 2015 by WH Allen

[ii] The Confidence Code by Katty Kay and Claire Shipma. Oublished in July 2015 by HarperCollins; International ed. edition

[iii] Bain.com – Everyday Moments Of Truth
https://www.bain.com/insights/everyday-moments-of-truth

[iv] Women and Confidence: An Alternative Understanding of the 'Confidence Gap'
https://internal.simmons.edu/~/media/Simmons/About/CGO/Documents/Leadership-Conference-Write-Up.ashx?la=en

[v] Appearing self-confident and getting credit for it: Why it may be easier for men than women to gain influence at work
https://faculty.insead.edu/natalia-karelaia/documents/Guillen%20Mayo%20Karelaia%202017%20Appearing%20self-confidence%20Gender%20In%20press.pdf

Chapter 1 - Why Don't I Feel Good Enough?

[vi] Meagan O'Reilly Ted Talk
https://www.youtube.com/watch?v=nUHDSGKfXmQ

Chapter 3 - The Inner Critical Parrot

[vii] Psychologist Rick Hanson – How to Stand Up To Your Inner Critic https://ideas.ted.com/how-to-stand-up-to-your-inner-critic/

[viii] The 7 Types of Inner Critic – Jay Earley and Rachel Weiss
https://personal-growth-programs.com/the-seven-types-of-inner-critics/

Chapter 4 - Perfectionism

[ix] Thomas Curran of Bath University and Andrew Hill of York University in their research – Perfectionism Is Increasing Over Time
https://www.apa.org/pubs/journals/releases/bul-bul0000138.pdf

[x] Hewitt and Flett (1991)
https://www.sciencedirect.com/science/article/pii/0191886994900736

[xi] Pauline C lance and Suzanne Imes
https://psycnet.apa.org/record/1979-26502-001

Chapter 5 - Imposter Syndrome

[xii] NatWest Research
https://www.telegraph.co.uk/business/women-entrepreneurs/imposter-syndrome-women-careers/

[xiii] Michael Neill www.michaelneill.org

[xiv] 5 Types of Imposter Syndrome – Dr Valerie Young
https://impostorsyndrome.com/5-types-of-impostors/

[xv] The Secret Thoughts of Successful Women: Why Capable People Suffer From the Imposter Syndrome and How to Thrive in Spite of It by Valerie Young. Published in October 2011by Crown Business

[xvi] https://www.themuse.com/advice/5-different-types-of-imposter-syndrome-and-5-ways-to-battle-each-one

Chapter 6 - Comparititis

[xvii] University of Pennsylvania published a study in the Journal of Social and Clinical Psychology University of Pennsylvania study, No More FOMO: Limiting Social Media Decreases Loneliness and Depression: https://guilfordjournals.com/doi/10.1521/jscp.2018.37.10.751

[xviii] The Social Comparison Theory
https://www.psychologytoday.com/gb/blog/valley-girl-brain/201902/why-we-can-t-stop-thinking-about-other-people-s-lives

[xix] The Comparison Trap, Rebecca Wenner
https://www.psychologytoday.com/gb/articles/201711/the-comparison-trap

[xx] Jordan Harbinger https://www.jordanharbinger.com/why-you-compare-yourself-to-other-people-and-how-to-stop/

Chapter 7 – Keeping Your Power

[xxi] Women speak less when they are outnumbered - Brigham Young University
https://www.sciencedaily.com/releases/2012/09/120918121257.htm

[xxii] **What Happened When I Started Speaking Up**

In Meetings

https://medium.com/athena-talks/what-happened-when-i-started-speaking-up-in-meetings-d5b8766f7ed6\

[xxiii] **Justice, Interrupted: The Effect of Gender, Ideology and Seniority at Supreme Court Oral Arguments**
https://www.ssrn.com/abstract=2933016

[xxiv] The Science Behind Interrupting
https://www.scmp.com/magazines/post-magazine/long-reads/article/2137023/science-behind-interrupting-gender-nationality

[xxv] Voice type and gender on subsequent leader emergence
https://journals.aom.org/doi/abs/10.5465/amj.2016.0148

Chapter 8 – Coming Out of The Shadows

[xxvi]Forget a Mentor, Find a Sponsor: The New Way to Fast-Track Your Career by Sylvia Ann Hewlett. Published in September 2013 by Harvard Business Review Press

[xxvii] **7 Ways to Raise Your Visibility - https://www.forbes.com/sites/elenabajic/2015/07/28/7-ways-to-raise-your-visibility-and-advance-your-career/#768354eb4ff1**

Chapter 9 – Develop Your Brand
[xxviii] Being You by Maggie Eyre – published in May 2019 by Exisle Publishing

[xxix] Brandyourself.com – A definitive guide to personal branding https://brandyourself.com/definitive-guide-to-personal-branding

[xxx] Firework Career Coaching Programme https://www.fireworkcoaching.com

[xxxi] Phyllis Weiss Haserot – How To Leave A Legacy Where You Work (Forbes) https://www.forbes.com/sites/nextavenue/2015/08/12/how-to-leave-a-legacy-where-you-work/#5abee4a1412c pwhaserot@pdcounsel.com

[xxxii] https://www.verywellmind.com/the-big-five-personality-dimensions-2795422

[xxxiii] CV examples https://www.glassdoor.co.uk/blog/cv-personal-statement-examples/

Chapter 10 – Self-Promotion

[xxxiv] Laurie Rudman University of West Jersey https://citeseerx.ist.psu.edu/viewdoc/download?doi=10.1.1.453.3587&rep=rep1&type=pdf

[xxxv] Tara Mohr, Playing Big https://www.taramohr.com/the-playing-big-book/

[xxxvii] Women's Bragging Rights' by Jessi Smith and Meghan Huntoon https://scholarworks.montana.edu/xmlui/bitstream/handle/1/9028/SmithJ_PWQ_dec14POSTPRINT_A1b.pdf;sequence=1

Chapter 11 – I'm Okay and You're Okay

[xxxviii] UK Violence Intervention and Prevention Centre – The 4 basic styles of communicationhttps://www.uky.edu/hr/sites/www.uky.edu.hr/files/wellness/images/Conf14_FourCommStyles.pdf\

[xxxix] A Bill of Assertive Rights – Manuel J Smith https://www.goodreads.com/quotes/490242-a-bill-of-assertive-rights-i-you-have-the-right

[xl] 'A Woman In Your Own Right' by Anne Dickson. Published in October 2012 (30th Anniversary Edition) by Quartet Books

[xli] Daniel Ames, Pushing Up to a Point: Assertiveness and Effectiveness in Leadership and Interpersonal Dynamics. https://www.sciencedirect.com/science/article/pii/S0191308 509000136

'Playing Big' by Tara Mohr. Published in March 2015 by Arrow

Chapter 12 – Having That Difficult Conversation and Dealing with Conflict

[xlii] Daisy Dowling 7 Tips for Difficult Conversations https://hbr.org/2009/03/7-tips-for-difficult-conversat

[xliv] University of Waterloo study https://www.ncbi.nlm.nih.gov/pubmed/?term=University+o f+Waterloo+Canada+apologize+women

Chapter 13 – Communicating with Power

[xlv] Amy Cuddy TED Talk https://www.ted.com/talks/amy_cuddy_your_body_languag e_shapes_who_you_are?language=en

[xlvi] https://www.ted.com/talks/amy_cuddy_your_body_languag e_shapes_who_you_are?language=en

[xlvii] https://www.mintel.com/press-centre/social-and-lifestyle/uk-women-half-as-confident-as-men-asking-for-payrises

[xlviii] McKinsey report 2018 – Women in The Workplace https://www.mckinsey.com/featured-insights/gender-equality/women-in-the-workplace-2018
[xlix] Susan Heathfield How to Ask For A Pay Rise https://www.agcareers.com/newsletters/HowtoaskforaPayRaise.htm

Chapter 15 – Work the Room

[l] Lou Adler, Performance Based Hiring https://www.linkedin.com/pulse/new-survey-reveals-85-all-jobs-filled-via-networking-lou-adler/

[li] Interviewsuccessformula.com

[lii] LinkedIn - 80% Of Professionals Consider Networking To Be Important To Career Success https://news.linkedin.com/2017/6/eighty-percent-of-professionals-consider-networking-important-to-career-success

[liii] Caroline Castrillon, Why women need to network differently https://www.forbes.com/sites/carolinecastrillon/2019/03/10/why-women-need-to-network-differently-than-men-to-get-ahead/#7204b03bb0a1

[liv] Kellogg School of Management, A network's gender composition and communication pattern predict women's leadership success https://www.pnas.org/content/116/6/2033

[lv] Tizana Casciaro - Learn to Love Networking

https://hbr.org/2016/05/learn-to-love-networking

Chapter 16 – Bouncing Back

[lvii] Courtney Ackerman, What Is Self-Worth and How Do We Increase It? https://positivepsychology.com/self-worth/

[lviii] Adam Sicinski, How to Build Self-Worth https://blog.iqmatrix.com/self-worth

[lix] Kirsten Neff, Self-Compassion https://self-compassion.org/the-three-elements-of-self-compassion-2/

Finally

[lix] Meir Kay, Self-worth. https://youtu.be/F2hc2FLOdhI